Life Together

THE **FAMILY** DEVOTIONAL

Life Together

THE
FAMILY
DEVOTIONAL

CWR

STEVE AND BEKAH LEGG

Contents

Introduction 7

Week 1: Fighting for the promise 10

Week 2: A long way from home 22

Week 3: A change of heart 34

Week 4: Going home 46

Week 5: The next generation 58

Week 6: A new country 70

Week 7: A new era 82

Week 8: A new family 94

Week 9: Getting started 106

Week 10: True happiness 118

Week 11: Freedom 130

Week 12: Transformation 142

Introduction

I wonder what the biggest promise anyone has ever made to you was? For me and Steve, it was probably the promises we made to each other on our wedding day: promises to always love and look after each other no matter what happens.

When our girls were small we had special services at church where we promised to teach them about Jesus. We knew then, and we know now, that there are hundreds of important things to teach our children before they grow up and leave home, but that there is nothing or no one more important for them to discover than God and His great love for them. When we think about what we hope for our children as they grow up, it's this: that they know deep within them how much they are loved by God, that they understand that He is for them and has a plan for their lives, and that they know they can always trust Him to be good. We'd like them to be kind, brave and generous too, but the most important thing is for them to know Jesus. If they follow Him, the other stuff will come along too.

That's why we wrote this book. We know that there are all sorts of things trying to get our attention – school, work, friendships, programmes on TV, social media and a whole load of other activities, and we want to help you take some moments each day, together as a family, to focus on the things that matter the most. We think this is important, we think you'll like it and we're really sure it will help you follow Jesus together as a family.

In this book we look at another family who followed God together: Isaac, Jacob and Joseph – three generations living out an incredible promise God had originally given Isaac's father, Abraham. The promise to bless the whole world through him. These three unlikely characters carry this promise through good times and bad times. It's a promise about their future, their children's future and the generations they'll never get to meet. It's a promise which, hundreds of years later, Jesus came to fulfil so that the whole world can get to know God and be part of His plan and His family. Later on, Paul, in his letter to the church in Galatia, explained what it means to live in the freedom of that promise and how to grow as followers of Jesus.

All of these people chose to follow God no matter how tough and scary things got, especially Jesus. When Jesus walked on earth, He too faced a choice – to do things God's way or short-cut everything and take the simple route. Jesus chose God's way, even though it would mean being betrayed by His friend, let down by His mates, rejected by the crowds and killed by the politicians.

It's tough sometimes following Jesus, and it takes a tough choice. A choice to get to know Him better, to listen for His voice, to spend time in His presence and to live out what you learn when you do. But it's a choice that means you too get to live in that incredible promise of God.

Our prayer for you over the next 12 weeks is that as a family you will grow closer together, that you will discover new things about each other as you meet with Jesus and deepen your relationship with God. We pray you will know God's presence with you not just as you do these devotions but in the details of every day, and that these 12 weeks will be the beginning of a lifetime of getting to know Jesus better, sharing your life with Him and following where He leads you.

Bekah

Two boys

Genesis 25:21–28

'Because Rebecca had no children, Isaac prayed to the
LORD for her. The LORD answered his prayer, and Rebecca
became pregnant. She was going to have twins, and before
they were born, they struggled against each other in her
womb. She said, "Why should something like this happen to
me?" So she went to ask the LORD for an answer.

    The LORD said to her,
    "Two nations are within you;
    You will give birth to two rival peoples.
    One will be stronger than the other;
    The older will serve the younger."

    The time came for her to give birth, and she had twin sons.
The first one was reddish, and his skin was like a hairy robe,
so he was named Esau. The second one was born holding on
tightly to the heel of Esau, so he was named Jacob. Isaac was
sixty years old when they were born.

    The boys grew up, and Esau became a skilled hunter,
a man who loved the outdoor life, but Jacob was a quiet
man who stayed at home. Isaac preferred Esau, because
he enjoyed eating the animals Esau killed, but Rebecca
preferred Jacob.'

Something to think about

We're starting to look at a story set way before Jesus was born; a part of history where we see the beginning of God's special people. And it begins with a prayer for a child by a man called Isaac who knows his wife, Rebecca, can't have children. God replies by giving her two children: Jacob and Esau.

These boys are twins, but they're nothing alike. Right from the beginning they are wriggling and fighting, even in their Mum's tummy, and as they grow up they will be interested in totally different things. But they're both God's answers to prayers, both special to their parents and both important.

Bekah says...

In my family, we all look alike, but we're very different. I always loved curling up with a book and reading, while my brother and sister loved to be out climbing mountains or surfing! And they're much taller than me, too. I'm the shortest in the family.

Something to talk about

• How are the people in your family similar or different?
• How do you know you're all equally precious?

Pray

Father God, thank You for designing each of us to be just who we are. Help us to know that our differences are what make us unique and special. Amen.

Selling the treasure

Genesis 25:29–34

'One day while Jacob was cooking some bean soup, Esau came in from hunting. He was hungry and said to Jacob, "I'm starving; give me some of that red stuff."...

Jacob answered, "I will give it to you if you give me your rights as the firstborn son."

Esau said, "All right! I am about to die; what good will my rights do me then?"

Jacob answered, "First make a vow that you will give me your rights."

Esau made the vow and gave his rights to Jacob. Then Jacob gave him some bread and some of the soup. He ate and drank and then got up and left. That was all Esau cared about his rights as the firstborn son.'

Something to think about

Life was different back when this story was happening. In those days, the first-born child was the special one. They would inherit everything the family owned. Esau was the eldest so he was born with this huge privilege. But on this day, when he was hungry, all he could think about was food. He didn't treasure this gift he had been given the day he was born.

We can be a bit like that. God gives each of us gifts the day we are born, but these are not necessarily lots of money or belongings. It might be that we are great at maths, or reading, or are good at making friends. It might be a musical talent, being a good listener or being very sporty. The problem is that sometimes we don't appreciate what we've been given. We'd rather have something else, or be like someone else, so we don't make the most of what God has given us – and that means we miss out.

Steve's amazing fact

Pirates are well-known for burying their treasure, although that wasn't always what they did. Some pirates wanted their share of the loot before they buried the treasure. And while we may think of gold and silver, a pirate's treasure was actually mostly food, wood, cloth and animal skins.

Something to talk about

· What gifts do you think God has given you?
· Have you ever wished you were more like someone else?

Pray

Dear Lord God, thank You for making us, us. Help us to know what our special gifts are and to use them well. Amen.

A promise to pass on

Genesis 27:1–4

'Isaac was now old and had become blind. He sent for his older son Esau and said to him, "My son!"

"Yes," he answered.

Isaac said, "You see that I am old and may die soon. Take your bow and arrows, go out into the country, and kill an animal for me. Cook me some of that tasty food that I like, and bring it to me. After I have eaten it, I will give you my final blessing before I die."'

Something to think about

Years before this story, God had promised Isaac's dad, Abraham, that he would have a special child. He told him that through this child, He would make a whole nation of more people than you could count, and these people would be God's special people. God said that He would save the whole world through them. Amazing!

This incredible promise was passed down to Isaac when his father died, and in this story, now that Isaac is getting old, he is getting ready to pass the promise on to Esau. Esau may have given away his birth rights for a bowl of soup, but this promise was worth way more – imagine being able to be part of God's amazing plan and carry His promise with you all the time!

Bekah says...

The thing is, we *do* get to be part of God's amazing plan to save the world, and we don't have to do a thing to earn it! If we choose to follow Jesus, then actually we can play a part in His plan to save the world by telling people all about Him and by choosing to live in a way that shows His love to everyone. How cool is that?

Steve's amazing fact

Every year Americans host a huge Thanksgiving Day Parade, which features floats and giant balloons of famous characters. In 1997, high winds sent a massive purple Barney dinosaur balloon onto a pointy lamppost and it exploded! It just shows that you can't always plan for the weather.

Something to talk about

· Have you ever been part of a plan to do something great for someone else?
· How did that feel?

Pray

Father God, thank You for Your promise all those years ago to have a plan to save the world, and thank You for sending Jesus to be the rescuer. Help us to be part of Your plan to show people Your great love. Amen.

Cheating

Genesis 27:5–10

*'While Isaac was talking to Esau, Rebecca was listening. So
when Esau went out to hunt, she said to Jacob, "I have just
heard your father say to Esau, 'Bring me an animal and cook
it for me. After I have eaten it, I will give you my blessing
in the presence of the Lord before I die.' Now, my son,"
Rebecca continued, "listen to me and do what I say. Go to
the flock and pick out two fat young goats, so that I can
cook them and make some of that food your father likes so
much. You can take it to him to eat, and he will give you his
blessing before he dies."'*

Something to think about

Now the story takes a bit of sinister turn. The twins' mum
has a favourite and it's not Esau. Even though Jacob has
already taken the birth rights from Esau, she has a plan to
get him the promise too. She plans to trick Isaac into giving
the promise to Jacob while Esau is out hunting for food for
his dad. That is seriously bad behaviour – but Jacob goes
along with it.

   This is a family that knows God and has a special promise
from Him, but even so are caught up in cheating, lying,
jealousy and stealing. It's a bit of a relief to see that the

families in the Bible aren't perfect. Sometimes we think families that follow God are all perfect and lovely, but the truth is we all struggle with wanting to put ourselves first – just like Rebecca and Jacob. It's good to admit our struggles, take them to God and ask Him to help us be more loving to each other.

Steve's amazing fact

A popular version of the story of Cinderella was written by Charles Perrault way back in the seventeenth century. In the story, Cinderella is treated awfully by her new step-family but has a happy ending when she marries the prince. And in Perrault's original version, Cinderella even forgives her step-sisters, and they marry handsome gentlemen from the prince's court.

Something to talk about

· Are there times in your family when you don't look all perfect and lovely?
· What could you do today to be kind to each other?

Pray

Father God, thank You for showing us that You can work with imperfect people just like us. Help us to be honest about our struggles, and to ask You to help us be more like You. Amen.

Disappointed

Genesis 27:30–35

'Isaac finished giving his blessing, and as soon as Jacob left, his brother Esau came in from hunting. He also cooked some tasty food and took it to his father. He said, "Please, father, sit up and eat some of the meat that I have brought you, so that you can give me your blessing."

"Who are you?" Isaac asked.

"Your elder son Esau," he answered.

Isaac began to tremble and shake all over, and he asked, "Who was it, then, who killed an animal and brought it to me? I ate it just before you came. I gave him my final blessing, and so it is his forever."

When Esau heard this, he cried out loudly and bitterly and said, "Give me your blessing also, father!"

Isaac answered, "Your brother came and deceived me. He has taken away your blessing."'

Something to think about

This is quite a story – imagine how disappointed Esau must have been. He'd spent all that time hunting for the perfect animal, cooked it to perfection and brought it to his dad, only to discover his brother Jacob had got there before him, pretended be him and received their dad's blessing. Esau had lost everything.

Bekah says...

Disappointment is horrible. Whether it's not getting the present you'd hoped for your birthday, seeing your team lose in a competition or being let down by a friend, it can feel like the end of the world. I can still remember what it felt like when I failed my first driving test (and my second). I was so sad, and I felt like I was rubbish. I had to work really hard to look at what was still good in my life and not just focus on what was bad and sad.

Steve's amazing fact

Author J.K. Rowling spent many nights writing out ideas for her books in coffee shops, and described herself then to be the biggest failure that she knew. But it was the way she handled and embraced her disappointment that paved the way for her amazing success. After many rejections, her books were eventually published.

Something to talk about

· When have you been very disappointed?
· How did you manage to get over it?

Pray

Lord Jesus, thank You that You never let us down and that even when times are hard, You still love us and look after us. Help us to look at the good things in life, not just at the bad. Amen.

Unintended consequences

Genesis 27:41–45

'Esau hated Jacob, because his father had given Jacob the blessing. He thought, "The time to mourn my father's death is near; then I will kill Jacob."

But when Rebecca heard about Esau's plan, she sent for Jacob and said, "Listen, your brother Esau is planning to get even with you and kill you. Now, my son, do what I say. Go at once to my brother Laban in Haran, and stay with him for a while, until your brother's anger cools down and he forgets what you have done to him. Then I will send someone to bring you back. Why should I lose both my sons on the same day?"'

Something to think about

Jacob may have got the gift and the promise, but he is about to discover that there are always consequences of our actions. Esau is very angry so Rebecca decides that Jacob should run away until his brother calms down. Jacob had thought he'd got everything he wanted, but now he can't even live safely with his family.

There are consequences of everything we do – good and bad. If we lie, it makes it hard for people to trust us in the future. If we save money, then we can buy nice things. If we hurt someone, they may not want to be our friend anymore. It can be easy to get so caught up in what we want right now that we forget about what might happen because of it. Thinking about the consequences can help us make much better decisions now.

Steve's amazing fact

Now here's a fascinating example of unintended consequences, especially if you're having difficulties with rodents. Most people who have problems with rats and mice will stop feeding their cats, assuming that this will encourage them to hunt more. Actually the opposite is true: well-fed cats are better hunters than hungry ones!

Something to talk about

- When has something you've done caused something to happen that you didn't expect?
- When has someone else changed your life?

Pray

God, help us to think about the things we do and what might happen because of them. Guide us to make wise decisions. Amen.

Something for the weekend

This week we've looked at a family who didn't treat each other well. Why not plan some fun family time? Everyone could choose a favourite activity to do together and then you could take it in turns to do those things.

A fresh start

Genesis 28:10–15

'Jacob left Beersheba and started toward Haran. At sunset he came to a holy place and camped there. He lay down to sleep, resting his head on a stone. He dreamt that he saw a stairway reaching from earth to heaven, with angels going up and coming down on it. And there was the Lord standing beside him. "I am the LORD, the God of Abraham and Isaac," he said. "I will give to you and to your descendants this land on which you are lying. They will be as numerous as the specks of dust on the earth. They will extend their territory in all directions, and through you and your descendants I will bless all the nations. Remember, I will be with you and protect you wherever you go, and I will bring you back to this land. I will not leave you until I have done all that I have promised you."'

Something to think about

Jacob had done some really bad things but God wasn't finished with him. He may have been a cheat and a thief, but God still had a better plan for his life. Even as Jacob is running away, God appears to him in a dream to remind him that He will never let him down, that He will keep His promise to give him more children and grandchildren than he could count and that through Jacob's descendants, the whole world would be blessed. That blessing is Jesus, who would eventually be born into Jacob's family centuries later.

How amazing to know that no matter what we do or how much we mess things up, God never changes, never breaks His promises and never leaves us! He is always there to help us put things right.

Steve's amazing fact

Apparently we all dream for around two hours each night – even though we might not remember any of these dreams. Experts have found that a person will usually have several dreams every night and each one of these usually lasts for five to twenty minutes. Over the course of your life, that's probably around six years of dreaming!

Something to talk about

• Who is always there for you, no matter what you do?
• How does that make you feel?

Pray

Father God, thank You for loving us so much, even when we let You down. We're sorry for the times we get things wrong – please help us to put things right and be more like You. Amen.

Finally!

Genesis 28:16–22

'Jacob woke up and said, "The LORD is here! He is in this place, and I didn't know it!" He was afraid and said, "What a terrifying place this is! It must be the house of God; it must be the gate that opens into heaven."

Jacob got up early next morning, took the stone that was under his head, and set it up as a memorial. Then he poured olive oil on it to dedicate it to God. He named the place Bethel. (The town there was once known as Luz.) Then Jacob made a vow to the LORD: "If you will be with me and protect me on the journey I am making and give me food and clothing, and if I return safely to my father's home, then you will be my God. This memorial stone which I have set up will be the place where you are worshipped, and I will give you a tenth of everything you give me."'

Something to think about

Finally! Jacob suddenly gets it. Up until now, Jacob has only been concerned about himself, getting what he wants and making sure he has more than his brother. He didn't really appreciate the promise of God, or how amazing it was that his family were so loved by God; he just wanted everything for himself. But after this dream, Jacob realises how awesome God is and how wonderful it is that he is known and looked after by Him. He even gets scared – God is bigger and more holy than he had ever imagined, and it's probably made him realise that he's just a little, naughty pipsqueak in comparison.

Bekah says...

It's like Jacob suddenly realised that God is more than someone you just go to with a list of things you want, and that actually the right way to come to God is by worshipping Him. He's right! Sometimes it's easy to forget just how awesome God is. Yes, He is our loving heavenly Father, and yes, Jesus can be our friend; but that is a pretty huge privilege of ours.

Something to talk about
· Do you sometimes forget how awesome God is?
· What amazes you about God?

Pray
Dear Lord God, You are bigger and better than we can imagine. You made everything we can see, and even things we can't see. You are totally awesome. Thank You for loving us. Amen.

Second chances

Genesis 29:9–14

'While Jacob was still talking with them, Rachel arrived with the flock. When Jacob saw Rachel with his uncle Laban's flock, he went to the well, rolled the stone back, and watered the sheep. Then he kissed her and began to cry for joy. He told her, "I am your father's relative, the son of Rebecca."

She ran to tell her father; and when he heard the news about his nephew Jacob, he ran to meet him, hugged him and kissed him, and brought him into the house. When Jacob told Laban everything that had happened, Laban said, "Yes, indeed, you are my own flesh and blood." Jacob stayed there a whole month.'

Something to think about

Even though Jacob finally understands that he needs to follow God, it's still not safe for him to go back home to his parents' house. So instead, he goes to his uncle's home. Here he gets an amazing welcome, even though he hadn't met them before. What a lovely, welcoming family. It's a bit like God's family. We are meant to be like Laban here – ready and delighted to welcome people in. All sorts of people; old or young, boys or girls, rich or poor.

Bekah says...

The churches in our town have worked really hard to be welcoming to all sorts of people, and in the last year we have welcomed two families from Syria who had lost their homes and were living in a refugee camp. They couldn't speak English, and they follow a different religion, but it has been great to welcome them into our church community and show them the love of Jesus.

Steve's amazing fact

A group of sheep is known as a herd, flock or mob. I once had to give a sheep a haircut on live TV. That's another story, but I had to learn a load of facts as part of the show. Did you know recent statistics show that 3 million people live in New Zealand, but they are outnumbered by the 60 million sheep there?

Something to talk about

· When has someone really welcomed you?
· Is there someone you could welcome into your family – even just for a meal?

Pray

Father God, thank You that You love to welcome people into Your family. Help us to be like You, and to help people feel at home with us. Amen.

In love

Genesis 29:16–20

'Laban had two daughters; the elder was named Leah, and the younger Rachel. Leah had lovely eyes, but Rachel was shapely and beautiful.

   Jacob was in love with Rachel, so he said, "I will work seven years for you, if you will let me marry Rachel."

   Laban answered, "I would rather give her to you than to anyone else; stay here with me." Jacob worked seven years so that he could have Rachel, and the time seemed like only a few days to him, because he loved her.'

Something to think about

Jacob has a serious crush. In fact, it's more than that – he has totally fallen in love with Rachel and wants to marry her. He's also learned that just taking what he wants isn't right, so this time he's ready to work for what he wants and earn the love of the woman he loves. He's not going to trick her into marriage, or force her, he's going to work for seven years so that she and her dad know just how serious he is about her. Impressive.

Bekah says...

We live in a world where we can get a lot of things at the click of a button, but the truth is, the most important things are worth working for. We have to work at school to help our brains grow, we help around the home to show love for our family, and we have to save our money to be able to buy special things. Sometimes, a bit like Jacob, we need to work and make sacrifices to make friends - we need to be caring, kind and trustworthy people in order to have good friendships.

Steve's amazing fact

Shirley Temple was a famous American actress who had a fascinating life and didn't wait around when it came to love. She and her husband-to-be knew each other for just 12 days before they got engaged, and stayed together for the next 55 years!

Something to talk about

· When have you had to work hard to earn something?
· When have you made a sacrifice for the people you love?

Pray

Father God, You gave Your Son so that we could be Your friends. That's so amazing! Help us to be like You and be ready to work for the people we love. Amen.

Tricked

Genesis 29:21–27,31–32

'Then Jacob said to Laban, "The time is up; let me marry your daughter." So Laban gave a wedding feast and invited everyone. But that night, instead of Rachel, he took Leah to Jacob... Not until the next morning did Jacob discover that it was Leah. He went to Laban and said, "Why did you do this to me? I worked to get Rachel. Why have you tricked me?"

Laban answered, "It is not the custom here to give the younger daughter in marriage before the elder. Wait until the week's marriage celebrations are over, and I will give you Rachel, if you will work for me another seven years."

When the LORD saw that Leah was loved less than Rachel, he made it possible for her to have children, but Rachel remained childless. Leah became pregnant and gave birth to a son. She said, "The LORD has seen my trouble, and now my husband will love me"; so she named him Reuben.'

Something to think about

Trickery seems to run in this family. Jacob has worked his seven years, and it's his wedding day. In comes the bride with a veil over her face, the wedding goes ahead and Jacob gets married. But the next day he realises it's the wrong sister! Uncle Laban was worried no one was going to marry Leah, so he sent her instead. Poor Jacob!

Actually, poor Leah too – imagine being made to marry someone who you knew wanted to marry someone else! This is a strange story in the Bible, and Leah has been treated terribly. It must seem like no one wants her or cares what she needs. But the truth is that God watches out for her and has a plan to give her lots of children for her to enjoy life with and be loved by.

Steve says...

Even when we're friends with God, tough things can happen to us. Sometimes it can feel as though we've got no friends, or that we're all alone. But God is always there, always loves us and will always look after us.

Something to talk about

· Has there been a time when you have felt all alone?
· What helped you when you were feeling like this?

Pray

Father God, thank You for always being there, even when it feels like other people aren't. Help us to always find comfort in Your friendship. Amen.

All paid up

Genesis 30:25–30

'Jacob said to Laban, "Let me go, so that I can return home. Give me my wives and children that I have earned by working for you, and I will leave. You know how well I have served you."

Laban said to him, "Let me say this: I have learned by divination that the LORD has blessed me because of you. Name your wages, and I will pay them."

Jacob answered, "You know how I have worked for you and how your flocks have prospered under my care. The little you had before I came has grown enormously, and the LORD has blessed you wherever I went. Now it is time for me to look out for my own interests."'

Something to think about

Jacob has changed. He's no longer the cheat and thief; he's become a hardworking, trustworthy man and he's ready to go home. He has worked 14 years for his uncle – which is longer than some of you have even been alive – his family has grown, and now he is ready to start building his own farm with his new family. Perhaps the most important change: he's ready to play his part in God's big story and the promise God had given to Abraham all those years ago.

There are things in all of us that God needs to work

on and help us change. We might not be cheats or thieves, but maybe we need to learn to be more patient, generous, hardworking or kind.

Bekah says...

When I was about 11, I was struggling with some of my friendships and I realised that it was partly because I sometimes talked about my friends behind their backs. I decided I wanted to change and become a really trustworthy person, and I asked God to help me. He did!

Something to talk about

· How have you made good changes in your life over the years?
· Are there things now that you'd like God to help you work on?

Pray

God, thank You that You have a plan to help us become more like You. We choose to let You work in our lives every day. Amen.

Something for the weekend

This week we talked about welcoming people in and making them at home, so perhaps you could invite someone different from school or church to your house for a play date, or even just a coffee and chat?

Waiting for God

Genesis 31:1–3,17–18

'Jacob heard that Laban's sons were saying, "Jacob has taken everything that belonged to our father. All his wealth has come from what our father owned." He also saw that Laban was no longer as friendly as he had been earlier. Then the LORD said to him, "Go back to the land of your fathers and to your relatives. I will be with you."

So Jacob got ready to go back to his father in the land of Canaan. He put his children and his wives on the camels, and drove all his flocks ahead of him, with everything that he had acquired in Mesopotamia.'

Something to think about

Jacob knew that he had changed, he knew that he had worked hard to create a family of his own, and now he knew that Uncle Laban and his children were not as friendly as they had once been. He wanted to go home, but he waited for God to tell him it was time. Jacob had learned to wait for God and do things His way.

Doing things God's way can be frustrating. Sometimes He has a different time scale to us, and sometimes He will make things happen in a different, unexpected way. Jacob had learned that it's best to wait for God and trust Him to know best.

Steve says...

Years ago, I made a children's cartoon called *It's a Boy!*, all about the Christmas story. I had great plans for it to take three months and be paid for quickly, but actually it took three years and £250,000 to get everything done. God had different plans to me, but they were still good.

Steve's amazing fact

You can't just plant a seed and expect it to grow in a day. The narrow-leafed campion plant usually flowers each summer, however, one particular narrow-leafed campion took more than 30,000 years to flower. That certainly took some patience.

Something to talk about

· When have you had to wait a long time for something to happen?
· How did that make you feel?

Pray

Father God, help us to remember that You know more than we do, and that Your plans are better than ours. Help us to trust You to know best. Amen.

Protected

Genesis 31:22–27

'Three days later Laban was told that Jacob had fled. He took his men with him and pursued Jacob for seven days until he caught up with him in the hill country of Gilead. In a dream that night God came to Laban and said to him, "Be careful not to threaten Jacob in any way." Jacob had set up his camp on a mountain, and Laban set up his camp with his relatives in the hill country of Gilead.

Laban said to Jacob, "Why did you deceive me and carry off my daughters like women captured in war? Why did you deceive me and slip away without telling me? If you had told me, I would have sent you on your way with rejoicing and singing to the music of tambourines and harps."'

Something to think about

Jacob was scared of Uncle Laban and his family so he ran away in the middle of the night, which made Laban very angry – he'd not even had a chance to say goodbye to his daughters. But God was watching out for Jacob and warned Laban not to hurt or even threaten him.

Laban learned that God was watching out for Jacob, but this was a lesson for Jacob to learn too. He didn't need to sneak out and run away. If God had told him to go home, then God would make sure he got home safely. Jacob didn't need to come up with his own safety plan, he could trust God to look out for him.

Bekah says...

When I was training to be a teacher, before I knew Steve or had children, God asked me to go and teach in Kenya. At first it seemed exciting, but then it got a bit scary – some serious incidents had gone on there and I started to think about changing my mind. But I was sure God had asked me to go, so I trusted Him to keep me safe. And He did.

Steve says...

One of my favourite verses is God talking to His friend Joshua: 'Don't be afraid or discouraged, for I, the LORD your God, am with you wherever you go' (Josh. 1:9).

Something to talk about

· When have you had do something scary?
· What helped you be brave?

Pray

Dear God, thank You that You have promised to always be with us. Help us to remember that, even when things are a bit scary. Amen.

In the right

Genesis 31:37–41

'Now that you have searched through all my belongings, what household article have you found that belongs to you? Put it out here where your men and mine can see it, and let them decide which one of us is right. I have been with you now for twenty years; your sheep and your goats have not failed to reproduce, and I have not eaten any rams from your flocks. Whenever a sheep was killed by wild animals, I always bore the loss myself. I didn't take it to you to show that it was not my fault. You demanded that I make good anything that was stolen during the day or during the night. Many times I suffered from the heat during the day and from the cold at night. I was not able to sleep. It was like that for the whole twenty years I was with you.'

Something to think about

Jacob was able to stand up for himself in front of Laban because he'd been making good choices for twenty years; the kind of choices he didn't make when he was a young man with his brother. It must have felt good to be able to stand and honestly say, 'I've done everything right. I haven't cheated, I've been good to you, I've worked hard for you and I've put myself out for you.'

Making good decisions can be really hard. Jacob says that sometimes it meant he was hot, other times it meant he was cold, and sometimes he went without sleep. But he made good choices anyway and now it means he can stand tall.

Bekah says...

In families, making good choices is often tough and sometimes means going without something you like. It might mean sharing your chocolate or toys, or taking it in turns to sit in the best chair, and it might mean not doing the thing you wanted when you wanted so you can help someone else.

Steve's amazing fact

It's been said that our brains make over 40,000 decisions every single day. Isn't that amazing? These might be tiny decisions like what we're going to watch on TV, or big decisions like what job we want to have.

Something to talk about

· When have you had to make a tough choice?
· What helped you decide?

Pray

Father God, help us to choose to be good, even when it doesn't seem like the most fun thing to do. Amen.

Making up

Genesis 31:51–55

'[Laban said] "Here are the rocks that I have piled up between us, and here is the memorial stone. Both this pile and this memorial stone are reminders. I will never go beyond this pile to attack you, and you must never go beyond it or beyond this memorial stone to attack me. The God of Abraham and the God of Nahor will judge between us." Then, in the name of the God whom his father Isaac worshipped, Jacob solemnly vowed to keep this promise. He killed an animal, which he offered as a sacrifice on the mountain, and he invited his men to the meal. After they had eaten, they spent the night on the mountain. Early the next morning Laban kissed his grandchildren and his daughters goodbye, and left to go back home.'

Something to think about

Laban and Jacob have had some serious disagreements, but they have worked them through and have managed to make up with each other. Now they are making a new agreement to not harm each other again, with a monument to remind them of this.

It's easy to fall out with people – friends or family – but it's harder to make up. Learning how to say sorry is one of the most important things we ever learn. So is working out how to make sure you don't fall out again.

Steve says...

God loves making up with us. Even though we mess up all the time, even when we've hurt other people, we can always come to Him and say sorry. Jesus paid the price for things we've done wrong when He died on the cross. So now we just have to come to God, admit what we've done and know He's done all the hard work to fix things with us.

Steve's amazing fact

The USSR and the USA had been enemies for decades, but on 19 November 1985, President Gorbachev and President Reagan shook hands and made it possible for their countries to be friends again.

Something to talk about

· When have you fallen out with someone?
· How did you make up?

Pray

Jesus, thank You that You have already done all the hard work to fix things with us. We're sorry for when we get things wrong. Amen.

Humbled

Genesis 32:9–12

'Then Jacob prayed, "God of my grandfather Abraham and God of my father Isaac, hear me! You told me, Lord, to go back to my land and to my relatives, and you would make everything go well for me. I am not worth all the kindness and faithfulness that you have shown me, your servant. I crossed the Jordan with nothing but a walking stick, and now I have come back with these two groups. Save me, I pray, from my brother Esau. I am afraid — afraid that he is coming to attack us and destroy us all, even the women and children. Remember that you promised to make everything go well for me and to give me more descendants than anyone could count, as many as the grains of sand along the seashore."'

Something to think about

What a change in Jacob! This is the man who used to think he should have everything, talking to God about not feeling like he deserves all he has. He knows that everything he has is a gift from God. He left his parents with nothing, and now he has a big family and lots of animals – and he's very grateful.

Jacob also knows that what he did to his brother Esau could mean he is still very angry, so he asks God to keep His promise and protect him and his family.

Bekah says...

I like that Jacob started his prayer by remembering all that God had done for him, before he talked about his worries. Sometimes our worries can seem enormous, but it is always good to stop and think about the good things that God has done for us. This often helps the worries seem smaller, and it always reminds us that God is there looking out for us.

Steve's amazing fact

Being worried has been described as feeling anxious about things that might happen. The word 'worry' actually comes from an old Anglo-Saxon word 'wyrgan,' which means to choke or strangle. Worrying is like a dog pulling while wearing a choke collar – the more they do it, the more it chokes.

Something to talk about

· Can you name three good things that have happened today?
· Is there one worry you'd like to ask God to help you with?

Pray

Father God, thank You for always keeping Your promises, and for always being good. Please protect us from the things that frighten us. Amen.

Making up. Again!

Genesis 32:17–21

'He ordered the first servant, "When my brother Esau meets you and asks, 'Who is your master? Where are you going? Who owns these animals in front of you?' you must answer, 'They belong to your servant Jacob. He sends them as a present to his master Esau. Jacob himself is right behind us.'" He gave the same order to the second, the third, and to all the others who were in charge of the herds: "This is what you must say to Esau when you meet him. You must say, 'Yes, your servant Jacob is right behind us.'" Jacob was thinking, "I will win him over with the gifts, and when I meet him, perhaps he will forgive me." He sent the gifts on ahead of him and spent that night in camp.'

Something to think about

When Jacob made up with Laban, he knew he'd done all the right things. It wasn't the same with Esau; Jacob knew he had treated Esau badly. So, he decides to give Esau some of his best and most valuable animals as a gift – a way of saying sorry, and a way to make up for his cheating.

Sometimes we need to show we're sorry. We might do this with words, or a hug, or it might be that we need to prove it with our actions – by changing our behaviour, or doing something to make it up to the person like helping with the washing up, tidying something away or even giving a present.

Steve says...

It's good to say sorry. Some big companies go to great lengths to publicise their apologies. In 2018, KFC, the Kentucky Fried Chicken people, published their apologies in full-page newspaper adverts when they ran out of chicken and had to close more than 600 stores across the UK.

Something to talk about

· Is there someone you need to say sorry to?
· What could you do to show you're sorry?

Pray

Lord God, thank You for loving us and always forgiving us. We're sorry for the things we've done wrong today. Please help us to make things right. Amen.

Something for the weekend

In Bible times, people often created special celebration meals and traditions to remember days when God was especially good. Why don't your family create a special meal and tradition to celebrate who you are and what God has done for you?

Wrestling

Genesis 32:23–30

'After he had sent them across, he also sent across all that he owned, but he stayed behind, alone.

Then a man came and wrestled with him until just before daybreak. When the man saw that he was not winning the struggle, he struck Jacob on the hip, and it was thrown out of joint. The man said, "Let me go; daylight is coming."

"I won't, unless you bless me," Jacob answered.

"What is your name?" the man asked.

"Jacob," he answered.

The man said, "Your name will no longer be Jacob. You have struggled with God and with men, and you have won; so your name will be Israel."

Jacob said, "Now tell me your name."

But he answered, "Why do you want to know my name?" Then he blessed Jacob.

Jacob said, "I have seen God face to face, and I am still alive"; so he named the place Peniel.'

Something to think about

This is a strange part of the story. What's it all about?

Until now, Jacob has struggled to do everything himself – he's cheated, conned and stolen what he wanted, then he learned to work for what he needed, and now finally God has come to show him that actually his biggest struggle of all is learning to admit he needs God. This struggle with God will show Jacob that God is stronger than him. When God wins the wrestling match, Jacob finally realises he is weak and needs God. He's then in a position to receive a blessing from God.

Bekah says...

God didn't come and wrestle with me in the night, but a couple of years ago, I did go through a whole lot of situations that were totally out of my control. It was a tough time, but through it I learnt that I'm not the answer to everything – God is.

Steve's amazing fact

Wrestling is probably the oldest sport on earth. There are cave drawings dating back to 3,000 BC showing people wrestling, and it's also one of the sports included in the ancient Olympic Games in Greece.

Something to talk about

· What are your weaknesses, the things you aren't very good at?
· Why not pray and ask God to be your strength in those areas?

Pray

Father God, thank You that You are bigger and stronger than anything we can imagine. Help us to remember that we don't have to struggle to do everything ourselves, because You are with us. Amen.

Reunited

Genesis 33:1–5

'Jacob saw Esau coming with his 400 men, so he divided the children among Leah, Rachel, and the two concubines. He put the concubines and their children first, then Leah and her children, and finally Rachel and Joseph at the rear. Jacob went ahead of them and bowed down to the ground seven times as he approached his brother. But Esau ran to meet him, threw his arms around him, and kissed him. They were both crying. When Esau looked around and saw the women and the children, he asked, "Who are these people with you?"

"These, sir, are the children whom God has been good enough to give me," Jacob answered.'

Something to think about

It's been twenty years since these brothers have seen each other, and a lot has changed – they have changed. Instead of fighting and hurting each other, these two men have remembered the most important thing: they love each other. Instead of trying to be better than his brother or fight him, Jacob bows to Esau. And Esau doesn't make him grovel; he hugs him and kisses him. It's beautiful.

You might not be able to imagine wanting to hug your brother or sister, but it's good to remember that behind the things that annoy us and wind us up, our families are really precious. Sometimes we need to remind ourselves of what is good about each other.

Bekah says...

I've become great friends with my brother and sister since we've grown up, but when we were young we often argued and fought. Back then I couldn't have imagined how much I'd enjoy spending time with them, but as I've got older I've realised they're fun, amazing people and I'm fortunate to have them.

Steve's amazing fact

They say a dog is man's best friend, but did you know that according to animal experts, horses, chimpanzees, elephants, baboons, hyenas, dolphins and bats can make friendships for life with animals from a different species?

Something to talk about

· Do you often argue with your family?
· What do you like about your family?

Pray

Dear God, help us to see the best in each other and to be able to put our disagreements behind us. Amen.

Forgiveness

Genesis 33:8–11

'Esau asked, "What about that other group I met? What did that mean?"

Jacob answered, "It was to gain your favour."

But Esau said, "I have enough, my brother; keep what you have."

Jacob said, "No, please, if I have gained your favour, accept my gift. To see your face is for me like seeing the face of God, now that you have been so friendly to me. Please accept this gift which I have brought for you; God has been kind to me and given me everything I need." Jacob kept on urging him until he accepted.'

Something to think about

The brothers are now almost arguing over who can be the kindest! But the important thing here is that Esau has chosen to forgive Jacob. He has every reason to stay angry with Jacob after all that he has done. Anyone would understand if he never wanted to see Jacob again or even made him pay back everything he took. But instead, Esau accepts Jacob's apology and they're able to make a fresh start.

Saying sorry is hard. But so is forgiving someone. Forgiving someone means letting go of what they did to you, choosing not to be angry about it anymore. It doesn't mean that what happened didn't matter, and it might not even mean you make friends – especially if someone is still trying to hurt you – it just means you choose to not want to get back at them or always hold it against them.

Bekah says...

Jesus set the most amazing example of forgiveness when He was dying on the cross. Even though He should never have been put there, even though people had been terribly unfair and hurt Him more than we can understand, He asked God to forgive them. Even on the cross, Jesus chose not be angry at what was happening to Him. And He did it all so we could be forgiven too. Amazing.

Something to talk about

· When has someone forgiven you for something big?
· How did that make you feel?

Pray

Father God, thank You for always being ready to forgive us when we come to You and say sorry for things we've done. Help us to be like You and forgive those around us. Amen.

Only God

Genesis 35:1–4

'God said to Jacob, "Go to Bethel at once, and live there.
Build an altar there to me, the God who appeared to you
when you were running away from your brother Esau."

So Jacob said to his family and to all who were with him,
"Get rid of the foreign gods that you have; purify yourselves
and put on clean clothes. We are going to leave here and
go to Bethel, where I will build an altar to the God who
helped me in the time of my trouble and who has been
with me everywhere I have gone." So they gave Jacob all
the foreign gods that they had and also the earrings that
they were wearing. He buried them beneath the oak tree
near Shechem.'

Something to think about

Jacob's family had been collecting things – little ornaments
and jewellery that they thought brought them luck or good
fortune. But those things weren't what had kept the family
safe, those things weren't what had helped Jacob change
into a great man, those things weren't what had helped him
build a big business. God had done that.

God wants Jacob to remember who the real God is, and
Jacob decides to get rid of anything else in his house that

distracted people from trusting God. We don't often have ornaments that we worship and think are gods, but we often have other things that we see as more important than God – games, gadgets and even our friends. It's important that we put God first in everything we do.

Steve says...

Over the years I've met and worked with lots of famous people. Of course it's exciting, but I soon came to realise that they are just people. Like anyone, they make mistakes and do things we may or may not agree with. At the end of the day, looking up to anybody, regardless of whether they are famous or not, isn't always good. Remember, the person that you look up to the most will probably let you down, because they're human. But God will never let you down.

Something to talk about

· What things are important in your life?
· How can you make sure these things don't end up more important to you than God?

Pray

God, You are amazing, better than anything or anyone else. We want to keep putting You first, so help us to see when we're being distracted by other things in our lives. Amen.

A new name

Genesis 35:9–15

'When Jacob returned from Mesopotamia, God appeared to him again and blessed him. God said to him, "Your name is Jacob, but from now on it will be Israel." So God named him Israel. And God said to him, "I am Almighty God. Have many children. Nations will be descended from you, and you will be the ancestor of kings. I will give you the land which I gave to Abraham and to Isaac, and I will also give it to your descendants after you." Then God left him. There, where God had spoken to him, Jacob set up a memorial stone and consecrated it by pouring wine and olive oil on it. He named the place Bethel.'

Something to think about

Jacob is finally ready to step into the promise and blessing he received from his dad all those years ago. God had first given him the name Israel after the wrestling in the night, but here He does it again. He then reminds Jacob that He will give him a great land and that his children will become whole nations of people.

Israel is a pretty important name; from that moment on, God's people would be called the Israelites and God's country would be called Israel. What an incredible mark to leave on the world.

Bekah says...

Jacob, or Israel as he became known, left an incredible legacy. By learning to follow and trust God and only God, he had the privilege of knowing that his children and his children's children would change the world. They would always have the job of pointing people to God and showing them who He was, and eventually Jesus would be born into their family, changing everything. I wonder what difference your life could make in the world...

Steve's amazing fact

Some buses in Israel have quotes from Leviticus 19:32 on them to encourage younger travellers to give up their seats for older people. This verse says, 'Show respect for old people and honour them'.

Something to talk about

· How would you like to change the world?
· How could you point people towards Jesus this week?

Pray

Father God, thank You that Your promise is not just for Jacob, it's for us too. Help us to know how we can point people to You. Amen.

Name change

Genesis 35:16–20

'Jacob and his family left Bethel, and when they were still some distance from Ephrath, the time came for Rachel to have her baby, and she was having difficult labour. When her labour pains were at their worst, the midwife said to her, "Don't be afraid, Rachel; it's another boy." But she was dying, and as she breathed her last, she named her son Benoni, but his father named him Benjamin.

When Rachel died, she was buried beside the road to Ephrath, now known as Bethlehem. Jacob set up a memorial stone there, and it still marks Rachel's grave to this day.'

Something to think about

This is a bit of a sad story. Rachel, the wife Jacob has loved for so long, dies giving birth. Jacob is very sad and sets up a stone to remember her by. But then he changes the name she gave to the baby. In her sadness, Rachel had called the baby Benoni, which means 'son of my sorrow'. Names meant a lot back then, and Jacob doesn't want this baby to be known by the sadness of that day – so instead he calls him Benjamin, meaning 'son who will be fortunate'. That's rather different isn't it?

Bekah says...

Everyone has sad days, and these can make us feel like the world will never be happy again. But our future does not have to be shaped by the sadness of our past. God says that He has a plan to give everyone hope and a future (Jer. 29:11). Even if today is sad or yesterday was terrible, we can still be blessed because of our God who loves us.

Steve's amazing fact

Did you know some cities in Japan have 'crying clubs' where people go to cry together? They reckon crying is so good for health that they sometimes even watch sad movies to get the tears flowing.

Something to talk about

· When have you had a very bad day?
· How did you turn the sadness into a blessing?

Pray

God, thank You that our sad days are not what shape our future; You shape our future. Thank You for having a plan for our lives. Amen.

Something for the weekend

This week we talked about living lives that change the world. Could you do something as a family that will make a change for somebody and point them towards Jesus? Maybe you could do something for a charity that makes a difference in the world.

Favouritism

Genesis 37:1–4

'Jacob continued to live in the land of Canaan, where his father had lived, and this is the story of Jacob's family.

Joseph, a young man of seventeen, took care of the sheep and goats with his brothers, the sons of Bilhah and Zilpah, his father's concubines. He brought bad reports to his father about what his brothers were doing.

Jacob loved Joseph more than all his other sons, because he had been born to him when he was old. He made a long robe with full sleeves for him. When his brothers saw that their father loved Joseph more than he loved them, they hated their brother so much that they would not speak to him in a friendly manner.'

Something to think about

We're moving on to a new generation of this family, but some things haven't changed much. Jacob has changed and grown up, but he hasn't learned that having favourites in a family just isn't fair. Joseph's coat is famous, people have written songs and even whole musicals about it, and he must have been over the moon with it. But it made his brothers sad. So sad that it left them hating Joseph.

Sometimes it's hard to know what we really feel. These

boys were just sad because of something their dad had done, but the way they dealt with it was by hating Joseph. The brothers didn't quite know how to show their sadness, so they bottled it up and it became anger instead.

Bekah says...

It's good to be able to talk about how you really feel and to be really honest. So often when we talk about issues, just saying them out loud makes things better and can help us to sort problems out before they get bigger and bigger.

Steve's amazing fact

A survey showed that the favourite sweet in a tin of Quality Street was The Purple One, and the least favourite is the blue Coconut Éclair. But there are always more Coconut Éclairs than there are of The Purple Ones in a tin.

Something to talk about

· Is there anything you're sad or worried about at the moment?
· What could others in your family do to help you feel better?

Pray

Father God, thank You for knowing everything about us, every thought in our heads. Help us to talk about how we feel with each other and with You. Amen.

Bragging

Genesis 37:5–8

'One night Joseph had a dream, and when he told his brothers about it, they hated him even more. He said, "Listen to the dream I had. We were all in the field tying up sheaves of wheat, when my sheaf got up and stood up straight. Yours formed a circle around mine and bowed down to it."

"Do you think you are going to be a king and rule over us?" his brothers asked. So they hated him even more because of his dreams and because of what he said about them.'

Something to think about

Joseph was having some pretty strange dreams. By the end of the story we'll realise that they were from God and that they predicted what would happen years in the future. But right now, Joseph is beginning to think that perhaps he has some special skills, and maybe he's going to be a special person. He's getting a pretty big head about it all and showing off about it to his brothers. It's not making him more popular, that's for sure!

It's great when we're good at something, and it's good to want to use our talents – we shouldn't pretend we don't have them. But showing off or bragging is never a good idea.

Bekah says...

We love to celebrate when one of our kids does really well at something, but we always have to remember that the others may struggle with that thing and so we're careful not to make one of them seem better than the others.

Steve's amazing fact

Nobody likes a show off, but have you heard of a humblebrag? It's all the rage on social media and is when someone tries to get away with bragging by making it look like they're not. It's now become a hashtag that people use, and here's one of my favourite examples: 'It's really weird being friends with famous people. You hardly ever get to see them and you have to schedule times to hang-out a week ahead.' Here's another classic: 'Argh! Just seen someone sitting opposite me on train is reading my book. Quite embarrassed. Watching for signs of enjoyment. He's frowning.'

Something to talk about

· What do you do more of, talking yourself up or talking others up?
· Take turns to tell each person with you now what is great about them.

Pray

Dear God, thank You for valuing all of us. Please help us to encourage each other and not try to make others feel less than us. Amen.

Stand up!

Genesis 37:18–22

'They saw him in the distance, and before he reached them, they plotted against him and decided to kill him. They said to one another, "Here comes that dreamer. Come on now, let's kill him and throw his body into one of the dry wells. We can say that a wild animal killed him. Then we will see what becomes of his dreams."

Reuben heard them and tried to save Joseph. "Let's not kill him," he said. "Just throw him into this well in the wilderness, but don't hurt him." He said this, planning to save him from them and send him back to his father.'

Something to think about

The brothers' anger has got seriously out of control. They have let their jealousy and their annoyance with Joseph turn into something really nasty. You can almost imagine them all winding each other up until they have got to this terrible point where they're planning to kill their own brother.

It can be so easy to get caught up with the crowd when people are being unkind, to just join in the mean conversations, but there's one brother who is brave enough to be different. Reuben doesn't get carried away with the crowd; he stands up for Joseph.

Bekah says...

It takes real courage to be different to a group of people; there can be a lot of pressure to join in and agree with them. It really matters that we learn to be brave and stand up for what we think is right, to say when we think people are being unkind and to stick up for people who need our support.

Steve's amazing fact

In 1963, Martin Luther King Jr. gave his famous *I Have a Dream* speech about the importance of civil rights to 250,000 people in America's capital. It became one of the most famous speeches in history and focused on his dream of a society where black people and white people live together in harmony.

Something to talk about

· Have you ever been part of a group of people who were being unkind about someone?
· How did that make you feel?

Pray

Father God, thank You for always doing what is right. Please help us to have the courage to be different and to stand up for what is good. Amen.

Dirty money

Genesis 37:23–28

'When Joseph came up to his brothers, they ripped off his long robe with full sleeves. Then they took him and threw him into the well, which was dry.

While they were eating, they suddenly saw a group of Ishmaelites travelling from Gilead to Egypt. Their camels were loaded with spices and resins. Judah said to his brothers, "What will we gain by killing our brother and covering up the murder? Let's sell him to these Ishmaelites. Then we won't have to hurt him; after all, he is our brother, our own flesh and blood." His brothers agreed, and when some Midianite traders came by, the brothers pulled Joseph out of the well and sold him for twenty pieces of silver to the Ishmaelites, who took him to Egypt.'

Something to think about

Reuben had planned to rescue Joseph and take him home, but Judah has a different idea – he doesn't want to kill Joseph either, but instead he sells him as a slave. Things are not looking good for Joseph.

I wonder what the brothers did with the money they made. The Bible doesn't tell us, but it's good to think about where things come from and how we spend our money.

It can be tempting to try to save money by buying cheap versions of things, but it's always good to check why things are so cheap – sometimes it's because somebody on the other side of the world has been working in a factory or a farm without being paid fairly, or even as a slave. Joseph's brothers made a very bad decision to sell their brother as a slave, let's make good decisions about what we buy and where it comes from.

Steve's amazing fact

Did you know that in West Africa, more than two million children work long, hard hours on cocoa plantations instead of going to school or playing with their friends? I love chocolate, but that makes me not want to eat it so much. The good news is, you can choose to buy chocolate that isn't made in this unfair way.

Something to talk about

· How do you choose what you buy?
· Do you ever check how and where things are made?

Pray

Dear Lord God, help us to remember that the decisions we make can have an effect on people we may never meet. Please show us how to make wise decisions about how we spend our money. Amen.

Cover up

Genesis 37:29–34

'When Reuben came back to the well and found that Joseph was not there, he tore his clothes in sorrow. He returned to his brothers and said, "The boy is not there! What am I going to do?"

Then they killed a goat and dipped Joseph's robe in its blood. They took the robe to their father and said, "We found this. Does it belong to your son?"

He recognized it and said, "Yes, it is his! Some wild animal has killed him. My son Joseph has been torn to pieces!" Jacob tore his clothes in sorrow and put on sackcloth. He mourned for his son a long time.'

Something to think about

Reuben wasn't there when his brothers sold Joseph, and he's not happy when he finds out. It's a terrible situation and no one wants to tell their dad, Jacob, what's gone on – so they make up a story to cover everything up. Poor Jacob is left thinking that Joseph has been killed by an animal.

Owning up to what we do wrong is hard, but it's so important to be truthful and deal with things. If the brothers had told Jacob and said sorry, maybe they could have got Joseph back. Instead, their fear of being found out stopped them from coming clean, and it really hurt their dad.

Bekah says...

Telling people we've done something wrong can be scary - what if they're cross with us? But making up a story and keeping it going is a horrible feeling, like we're living with a secret. The truth can be hard to tell, but once it's done you feel much better.

Steve's amazing fact

Two men got themselves into a lot of trouble after they had too much to drink and stole a penguin called Dirk from Sea World in Australia. When they woke up the following day they tried to look after him by feeding him and putting him in the shower, before releasing Dirk into a canal. Dirk was eventually rescued and returned to Sea World unharmed.

Something to talk about

· What's the hardest thing you've ever had to own up to?
· How did you feel once you'd done it?

Pray

Father God, we're sorry for the things we do wrong. Help us to be brave enough to tell the truth so we can sort things out. Amen.

Next to me

Genesis 39:1–6

'Now the Ishmaelites had taken Joseph to Egypt and sold him to Potiphar, one of the king's officers, who was the captain of the palace guard. The LORD was with Joseph and made him successful. He lived in the house of his Egyptian master, who saw that the LORD was with Joseph and had made him successful in everything he did. Potiphar was pleased with him and made him his personal servant; so he put him in charge of his house and everything he owned. From then on, because of Joseph the LORD blessed the household of the Egyptian and everything that he had in his house and in his fields. Potiphar handed over everything he had to the care of Joseph and did not concern himself with anything except the food he ate.'

Something to think about

While the brothers are cooking up stories at home, Joseph has been taken to Egypt. He's far from home and everyone he knows, but he's not alone. God is with him. This is a great part of the story. It would have been easy for Joseph to give up hope as he was carted away by the Ishmaelites, but instead he discovers there is nowhere you can go where God isn't with you. Joseph realises that even when your family turn on you, God is always there.

Steve says...

I have travelled all around the world, and one of the things that has helped me when I've been a bit homesick is knowing that even though Bekah and the girls are far away, God is always with me.

Something to talk about

· When have you felt really scared?
· What difference does knowing that God is always with you make to your life?

Pray

God, thank You that You are always with us and will never abandon us. Help us to remember that we are never really alone. Amen.

Something for the weekend

This week we thought about buying our food and clothes carefully – why don't you look out in the supermarket for food that is Fairtrade and then cook a lovely meal or bake a cake with it? It can be your 'no slavery meal' or 'no slavery cake'.

Good choices

Genesis 39:6–10

'Joseph was well-built and good-looking, and after a while his master's wife began to desire Joseph and asked him to go to bed with her. He refused and said to her, "Look, my master does not have to concern himself with anything in the house, because I am here. He has put me in charge of everything he has. I have as much authority in this house as he has, and he has not kept back anything from me except you. How then could I do such an immoral thing and sin against God?" Although she asked Joseph day after day, he would not go to bed with her.'

Something to think about

Imagine you'd been sold by your brothers, taken to a foreign land and made to work as a slave. Most people would be a bit grumpy. They may not try their best at their new job. They might sit and sulk, or just cry in a corner. But there's something different about Joseph – he's a hard worker and he tries to do good in any situation. So when the boss' wife thinks he looks rather handsome and starts to pay him a bit too much attention, he makes a wise decision to stay well clear!

Bekah says...

When life's not fair, it can be easy to get a bad attitude and tell ourselves that it's OK to do something naughty because of what's happened to us. We still need to make good choices, no matter what has happened or how unfair life seems. God made us to be like Him, and it's good to try to be like Him everywhere we go.

Steve's amazing fact

Bethany Hamilton is an amazing surfer from Hawaii who lost her arm in a vicious shark attack. You'd think she'd be terrified of going back into the water, but instead she went back to surfing after just one month. She learned to surf with one arm and, two years after the attack, went on to win a national surfing competition. Her amazing story is the subject of the film *Soul Surfer*.

Something to talk about

· When has life seemed pretty unfair to you?
· How did you react to this?

Pray

Father God, thank You that You are good all the time. Help us to be kind and wise like You, whatever situation we're in. Amen.

Another lost coat!

Genesis 39:11–20

'But one day when Joseph went into the house to do his work, none of the house servants was there. She caught him by his robe and said, "Come to bed with me." But he escaped and ran outside, leaving his robe in her hand. When she saw that he had left his robe and had run out of the house, she called to her house servants and said, "Look at this! This Hebrew that my husband brought to the house is insulting us. He came into my room... but I screamed as loud as I could. When he heard me scream, he ran outside, leaving his robe beside me."

She kept his robe with her until Joseph's master came home. Then she told him the same story: "That Hebrew slave that you brought here came into my room and insulted me. But when I screamed, he ran outside, leaving his robe beside me."

Joseph's master was furious and had Joseph arrested and put in the prison where the king's prisoners were kept, and there he stayed.'

Something to think about

Potiphar's wife liked to get her own way. So the fact that Joseph keeps turning her down makes her really mad! Poor Joseph has done nothing wrong, but he's in trouble anyway.

This time he's ended up in prison. We've all met people a bit like Potiphar's wife – who throw a tantrum when they don't get what they want. Maybe we do it ourselves sometimes. Do you get cross if someone says that you can't have some sweets or a biscuit, or that it's time to do your homework or turn the TV off?

Part of growing up is learning that sometimes we can't do what we want to do, and that doesn't automatically mean that people are being mean to us.

Bekah says...

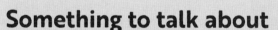

Our youngest daughter used to have the worst tantrums. She would shout and scream for what seemed like hours over the silliest things. Then, we realised it only happened if she was hungry. We made sure she ate more often and the tantrums stopped. Phew!

Something to talk about

· When have you really wanted something but not been able to have it?
· How do you react when people say 'no' to you?

Pray

Dear God, help us to know we're still loved even when people say 'no' to us. Please show us how to keep control of our tempers. Amen.

Strange dreams

Genesis 40:8–13

'They answered, "Each of us had a dream, and there is no one here to explain what the dreams mean."

"It is God who gives the ability to interpret dreams," Joseph said. "Tell me your dreams."

So the wine steward said, "In my dream there was a grapevine in front of me with three branches on it. As soon as the leaves came out, the blossoms appeared, and the grapes ripened. I was holding the king's cup; so I took the grapes and squeezed them into the cup and gave it to him."

Joseph said, "This is what it means: the three branches are three days. In three days the king will release you, pardon you, and restore you to your position. You will give him his cup as you did before when you were his wine steward.'

Something to think about

Joseph is still holding on to that great attitude and so he starts to get a good reputation in the prison. He's given some extra responsibilities, which allows him to meet two new prisoners: a baker and a wine taster for the king. They're desperate to find out what their dreams mean and Joseph spots an opportunity to show them how great God is.

Joseph's gift of interpreting dreams is amazing, and at this point he could just use it to make himself some new friends. Instead, he chooses to tell these men that it's not him who is special, it's God. Joseph just gets more and more impressive! Despite all that's happened to him, he still loves God and wants God to get the glory for what He does through Joseph.

Steve says...

I've always loved magic, ever since I watched a magician called Paul Daniels on TV when I was a boy. I remember being blown away when he made an elephant disappear into thin air (or so it seemed!). This love for magic has meant I've spent my life travelling the world, using my magic skills to tell people about Jesus.

Something to talk about

· What amazing talents have you got?
· How can you use them to tell people about God?

Pray

Father God, thank You for giving us all special talents. Help us to know how we can use them to tell people about You. Amen.

Forgotten

Genesis 40:14,20–23

'[Joseph said] "But please remember me when everything is going well for you, and please be kind enough to mention me to the king and help me get out of this prison."

On his birthday three days later the king gave a banquet for all his officials; he released his wine steward and his chief baker and brought them before his officials. He restored the wine steward to his former position, but he executed the chief baker. It all happened just as Joseph had said. But the wine steward never gave Joseph another thought — he forgot all about him.'

Something to think about

Joseph's dream interpreting was accurate – three days later, the wine steward is back at work, and the baker... well his story doesn't end so well. We can understand why the baker doesn't tell anyone about the guy who'd interpreted his dreams in prison, it's hard to speak in his position! But the steward has no excuse – he's just flat out forgotten Joseph and gets back on with living his own life.

It can be very easy to overlook the people we come across as we get busy looking out for ourselves. It's not that we mean to be selfish, we just forget. So sometimes we need to be reminded to keep an eye out for people we can help along the way – people at school, or at work or even someone we pass on the street. Taking a moment to be kind can make a huge difference for someone.

Bekah says...

When our girls were little, it was hard work taking them out and about in town. I remember travelling to London one time with two babies and struggling to get around with their big pram. I was so grateful when people stopped to help me get them up and down the stairs in the train stations, it was really kind.

Steve says...

It's amazing how a simple random act of kindness can totally change someone's day. How about giving someone a compliment today? You could even write it down. It costs nothing, takes hardly any time, and could make someone's entire day. Don't just think it, say it.

Something to talk about

· When has someone gone out of their way to do something kind for you?
· When have you done something kind for someone else?

Pray

Dear Lord God, You are always kind and loving, and You don't forget anyone. Help us to find someone to help today. Amen.

A long wait

Genesis 41:1–8

'After two years had passed, the king of Egypt dreamed that he was standing by the River Nile, when seven cows, fat and sleek, came up out of the river and began to feed on the grass. Then seven other cows came up; they were thin and bony. They came and stood by the other cows on the riverbank, and the thin cows ate up the fat cows. Then the king woke up. He fell asleep again and had another dream. Seven ears of corn, full and ripe, were growing on one stalk. Then seven other ears of corn sprouted, thin and scorched by the desert wind, and the thin heads of grain swallowed the full ones. The king woke up and realized that he had been dreaming. In the morning he was worried, so he sent for all the magicians and wise men of Egypt. He told them his dreams, but no one could explain them to him.'

Something to think about

Waiting is no one's favourite thing. We've already thought about times when we want something but we're told 'no', and today we're thinking about having to wait for a 'yes', which is slightly better but still tough! Two years have passed in our story and Joseph is still in prison. That is a very long, difficult wait for things to get better.

Meanwhile, the king has been having some weird dreams. It could just be something he's eaten, but he thinks these dreams mean something, and no one can tell him what! Could God be at work while Joseph the 'dream interpreter' is waiting?

Bekah says...

One of the longest waits in my life was pregnancy! I was so excited each time I realised I was going to have a baby, but I had to wait months and months to meet my girls. In fact, I had to wait months to even know they were girls - months of getting bigger, feeling uncomfortable and needing a wee all the time. But the wait was totally worth it because I had my beautiful girls at the end of it all.

Something to talk about

· What might have helped Joseph for those two years in prison?

· When have you waited a long time for something that's been totally worth it?

Pray

Father God, show us how to be patient and good at waiting happily for things when we can't have them straight away. Amen.

Oops!

Genesis 41:9–14

'Then the wine steward said to the king, "I must confess today that I have done wrong. You were angry with the chief baker and me, and you put us in prison in the house of the captain of the guard. One night each of us had a dream, and the dreams had different meanings. A young Hebrew was there with us, a slave of the captain of the guard. We told him our dreams, and he interpreted them for us. Things turned out just as he said: you restored me to my position, but you executed the baker."

The king sent for Joseph, and he was immediately brought from the prison. After he had shaved and changed his clothes, he came into the king's presence.'

Something to think about

Finally, things are starting to look a little bit better for Joseph! He may have felt left behind, but God hasn't forgotten him. God seems to have reminded the wine steward about Joseph too as he realises Joseph might be just who the king needs to explain his dreams. Joseph is brought to the king, and is given some new clothes and a chance to freshen up, ready to be useful.

Our friends can let us down, even when we've been really good to them. When this happens, it's hard to not just feel grumpy about it all, but it helps to remember that just like He was with Joseph all those years ago, God is in control. He hasn't forgotten us, and anything is possible.

Steve's amazing fact
Did you know it's highly likely that animals dream too? Have you ever watched your pet dog or cat sleep and seen that they were moving their paws and making noises like they were chasing something?

Something to talk about
· When has someone else telling the truth helped you?
· How difficult do you find it to admit mistakes?

Pray
God, thank You that You always have a plan for our lives, even when the world around us seems tough. Help us to wait patiently like Joseph to see what You will do. Amen.

Something for the weekend
This week we looked at being patient and how Joseph waited patiently in prison, trusting that God would work things out. Around the world, there are people in prison just because they follow Jesus. Why don't you have a look at a website like opendoorsuk.org and see how you can pray for or encourage these people?

Serving the king

Genesis 41:15–16,28–32

'The king said to him, "I have had a dream, and no one can explain it. I have been told that you can interpret dreams."

Joseph answered, "I cannot, Your Majesty, but God will give a favourable interpretation."

"It is just as I told you — God has shown you what he is going to do. There will be seven years of great plenty in all the land of Egypt. After that, there will be seven years of famine, and all the good years will be forgotten, because the famine will ruin the country. The time of plenty will be entirely forgotten, because the famine which follows will be so terrible. The repetition of your dream means that the matter is fixed by God and that he will make it happen in the near future."'

Something to think about

Joseph's world has totally changed and this is a make or break moment. He's out of prison for the first time in years and he's standing in front of one of the most important men in the world. He has a chance to turn his life around and make himself irreplaceable to the king. But that's not where he starts.

Joseph started as a boy with a big head, but he has come a long way. On the journey he has discovered just how amazing God is, and how he is nothing without God. So he tells the king that it's not him he needs, it's God, and then he goes on to explain this really important dream.

Bekah says...

What a change! God loves everyone, but He loves to transform us into better versions of ourselves, just like He did with Joseph. I love watching people change as they get to know Jesus - becoming kinder, braver, more patient and less selfish. And I love looking back and seeing how God has changed me.

Steve's amazing fact

Chameleons are colourful lizards that can change their skin colour. According to experts at the San Diego Zoo, a chameleon's skin changes colour because of changes in light, temperature or humidity, or because it's angry or scared.

Something to talk about

· How have you seen God change you?
· Are there other parts of your life you'd like God to help you with?

Pray

Dear God, we want to be more like You every day. Help us to see where You can help us change. Amen.

A great plan

Genesis 41:33–38

"'Now you should choose some man with wisdom and insight and put him in charge of the country. You must also appoint other officials and take a fifth of the crops during the seven years of plenty. Order them to collect all the food during the good years that are coming, and give them authority to store up corn in the cities and guard it. The food will be a reserve supply for the country during the seven years of famine which are going to come on Egypt. In this way the people will not starve."

The king and his officials approved this plan, and he said to them, "We will never find a better man than Joseph, a man who has God's Spirit in him."'

Something to think about

Wow! What an amazing turnaround. Joseph has been loyal and faithful to God, and he has taken his good attitude everywhere he has gone. He's passed on God's wisdom to the king, which means that the king, the most important man in Egypt, recognises that Joseph is special because God is with him. It also means that even though Egypt is about to have a famine, God has been able to provide a plan for how to survive it.

Bekah says...

When we stay loyal and faithful to God wherever we go, and bring His wisdom to the conversations we have, then we can make a real difference in the world. We probably won't be recognised by kings, but we can help to bring love and kindness to people who need it.

Steve's amazing fact

The Queen's Honours lists are published twice a year, at New Year and in mid-June on the Queen's official birthday. The list contains a wide variety of people from different backgrounds, from celebrities and sporting stars to business people and dinner ladies. Honours are given to people from all walks of life who have made a difference to their community, and are usually presented by a senior member of the Royal Family. What an honour!

Something to talk about

· When have you been able to make a big difference in someone's life?
· How did that feel?

Pray

Dear God, help us to spot those moments when we can make a difference, and teach us to show Your love and kindness everywhere we go. Amen.

For such a time

Genesis 41:39–44

'The king said to Joseph, "God has shown you all this, so it is obvious that you have greater wisdom and insight than anyone else. I will put you in charge of my country, and all my people will obey your orders. Your authority will be second only to mine. I now appoint you governor over all Egypt." The king removed from his finger the ring engraved with the royal seal and put it on Joseph's finger. He put a fine linen robe on him, and placed a gold chain around his neck. He gave him the second royal chariot to ride in, and his guard of honour went ahead of him and cried out, "Make way! Make way!" And so Joseph was appointed governor over all Egypt. The king said to him, "I am the king — and no one in all Egypt shall so much as lift a hand or a foot without your permission."'

Something to think about

Who would have thought that Joseph could end up with a job like this? He started as a big-headed little brother, got sold as a slave, ended up in prison and now is second only to the king. What a journey – in prison one day and in charge of the country the next. God can do amazing things with our lives, no matter what mistakes we make or how tough things get. Joseph ended up in just the right place at just the right time to be able to save a whole country from starving when the famine came. Incredible!

Bekah says...

I've had all sorts of jobs, lived in different countries and got married twice. My family is a muddly one, with different parents and even foster children. It can seem like there have been mistakes and muddles and messes, but when I look back I can see that God has been at work, bringing everyone together to work for His good. He's great.

Something to talk about

· When have you seen God turn a difficult situation into something amazing?
· Do you have a situation now that you'd like to ask God to turn around?

Pray

Father God, thank You for having a plan that is the bigger than we can see. Help us to know that You have everything under control, and to feel safe with You. Amen.

A new life

Genesis 41:46–52

'Joseph was thirty years old when he began to serve the king of Egypt. He left the king's court and travelled all over the land. During the seven years of plenty the land produced abundant crops, all of which Joseph collected and stored in the cities. In each city he stored the food from the fields around it. There was so much corn that Joseph stopped measuring it — it was like the sand of the sea.

Before the years of famine came, Joseph had two sons by Asenath. He said, "God has made me forget all my sufferings and all my father's family"; so he named his first son Manasseh. He also said, "God has given me children in the land of my trouble"; so he named his second son Ephraim.'

Something to think about

Joseph's life really has changed – he's got a wife now and children, and the names he gives these children show that God has given him so much that he has left his troubles behind. It's what God loves to do. Jesus said that choosing to follow Him is like being born all over again – starting a whole new life.

We can go through tough times, when it feels like nothing will ever be the same again, but God is the God of fresh starts and new beginnings, and He wants us to follow Him so that we can reach a place where we forget our troubles too.

Bekah says...

I can remember having some really tough times with friendships at school. I thought no one liked me, and that no one ever would. It was really lonely. Some days it felt like the only friend I had was Jesus. But, over time everything changed and God gave me so many great gifts that it's now hard to believe I used to get so sad about it all.

Steve's amazing fact

Dory is a cheerful Regal Blue Tang in the movies *Finding Nemo* and *Finding Dory* who suffers from short-term memory loss. In the films she forgets conversations within minutes of having them and is terrible with directions. Her condition is actually called anterograde amnesia.

Something to talk about

· Can you think of a tough time you have been through that now seems like it never happened?
· How did you get through it?

Pray

Dear Lord God, thank You for carrying us through tricky situations, and for always being our friend and giving us great gifts. Amen.

Provision

Genesis 42:1–5

'When Jacob learned that there was corn in Egypt, he said to his sons, "Why don't you do something? I hear that there is corn in Egypt; go there and buy some to keep us from starving to death." So Joseph's ten half-brothers went to buy corn in Egypt, but Jacob did not send Joseph's full-brother Benjamin with them, because he was afraid that something might happen to him.

The sons of Jacob came with others to buy corn, because there was famine in the land of Canaan.'

Something to think about

So, it isn't just Egypt who are having a famine, it's spread to Canaan where Joseph's brothers and family live. They hear about all the grain stored up in Egypt, and Jacob sends the boys to see if they can buy some food. He keeps Benjamin home with him because now that he thinks Joseph is dead, Benjamin is his youngest, most precious son.

We haven't read about Jacob for a while, this man with God's special promise, but God hasn't forgotten him. He has a plan to keep His promise and take care of this family even though they haven't been perfectly behaved. It's reassuring when you think about it – none of our families are perfect, none of us are perfect, we all make mistakes and let each other and God down. But that doesn't stop God loving us and looking out for us.

Bekah says...

When Jesus was talking to his friends, He told them they never needed to worry about what they would eat or what they would wear. He reminded them that He looks after everything – even the birds can trust Him to look after them (Matt. 6:26).

Steve's amazing fact

Did you know that wheat is the most grown cereal grain? Of all the land in the world that is used to grow crops, wheat is grown on 17% of this. And for good reason – whole grains are still the main type of food for about 35% of the world's population, and people have been eating the stuff for more than 17,000 years!

Something to talk about

· When has God provided for your family?
· Is there something you need to ask God for today?

Pray

Father God, thank You for being trustworthy, and thank You that You will always provide what we need when we need it. Amen.

Tested

Genesis 42:8–14,17

'Although Joseph recognized his brothers, they did not recognize him. He remembered the dreams he had dreamed about them and said, "You are spies; you have come to find out where our country is weak."

"No, sir," they answered. "We have come as your slaves, to buy food. We are all brothers. We are not spies, sir, we are honest men... We were twelve brothers in all, sir, sons of the same man in the land of Canaan. One brother is dead, and the youngest is now with our father."

"It is just as I said," Joseph answered. "You are spies. This is how you will be tested: I swear by the name of the king that you will never leave unless your youngest brother comes here. One of you must go and get him. The rest of you will be kept under guard until the truth of what you say can be tested. Otherwise, as sure as the king lives, you are spies."

Then he put them in prison for three days.'

Something to think about

What an awkward moment! The brothers are in front of Joseph, who they sold as a slave, but don't even realise it. Joseph realises that this is what that dream was about all those years ago when the stars bowed down to him. He's wise enough nowadays not to mention it. Instead, he decides to test them to see if he can trust them, which was also wise.

It's really good to make up with friends and family we've fallen out with, but it's also good to be careful so that people don't take advantage of us.

Something to talk about

· When have you fallen out and made up with a friend?
· Afterwards, how could you tell they had changed and were truly sorry?

Pray

Dear God, thank You for always giving us a second chance. Please help us to be wise in our friendships, and to be good friends to others. Amen.

Something for the weekend

We've been looking at how God flipped Joseph's life around and has now given him authority over Egypt. But having authority isn't always easy. Think about the leaders in your church. As a family, make a plan for something you could do to bless them this weekend, then do it!

Regret

Genesis 42:18–22

'On the third day Joseph said to them, "I am a God-fearing man, and I will spare your lives on one condition. To prove that you are honest, one of you will stay in the prison where you have been kept; the rest of you may go and take back to your starving families the corn that you have bought. Then you must bring your youngest brother to me. This will prove that you have been telling the truth, and I will not put you to death."

They agreed to this and said to one another, "Yes, now we are suffering the consequences of what we did to our brother; we saw the great trouble he was in when he begged for help, but we would not listen. That is why we are in this trouble now."

Reuben said, "I told you not to harm the boy, but you wouldn't listen. And now we are being paid back for his death."'

Something to think about

Joseph is harsh with his brothers, but he still gives them a way and a chance to fix things. Simeon stays behind in prison, while the others go off to get their younger brother. But they are beside themselves and are full of regret. They don't know this is Joseph; they don't know that this really is because of what they did. But they do know that they wish they'd never tried to hurt him, and they feel like this is what they deserve for what they did all those years ago.

Regret is when we wish we'd done something differently. It might be something we did that we really wish we hadn't, or something we wish we had done but didn't. It's a horrible feeling, but the wonderful thing is that even though we can't change the past, we can find forgiveness from Jesus and let Him take away the bad feeling.

Steve says...

Thinking before you act can help you make good choices and avoid feeling regret. It's always worth stopping and being sure you're going to be happy tomorrow, next week or even next year with your decision.

Something to talk about

• When have you done something you really regretted?
• What do you wish you had done differently?

Pray

Father God, we don't want to live with lots of regrets in our lives. Please help us to make wise decisions and to know Your forgiveness when we need it. Amen.

Responsibility

Genesis 43:6–9

'Jacob said, "Why did you cause me so much trouble by telling the man that you had another brother?"

They answered, "The man kept asking about us and our family, 'Is your father still living? Have you got another brother?' We had to answer his questions. How could we know that he would tell us to bring our brother with us?"

Judah said to his father, "Send the boy with me, and we will leave at once. Then none of us will starve to death. I will pledge my own life, and you can hold me responsible for him. If I do not bring him back to you safe and sound, I will always bear the blame."'

Something to think about

Jacob can't believe that he might now lose another son – two in fact. Simeon is in prison and now the brothers have told him they have to take Benjamin to Egypt if they are to get any more food and get Simeon back.

But these guys have changed. They are now telling the truth to their father about all that is happening, and Judah is taking responsibility for what happens next. He doesn't try to blame the mean man in Egypt or shout that it's all unfair. He just works out what needs to happen and says if it goes wrong, it's on him. Taking responsibility for our actions is hard, but these guys have learned the hard way that it's best.

Bekah says...

We've had a little boy live with us who found it really hard to take responsibility for what he does, partly because he used to get in a lot of trouble when he did something wrong. But we've been teaching him that it's good to own up. He thinks we're crazy – we high five him when he admits he's done something wrong. We don't like what he did, but we *love* that he was brave enough to be truthful about it.

Steve's amazing fact

The first ever successful heart transplant was performed on 3 December 1967 by Dr Christiaan Barnard in a hospital in South Africa. It was an amazing step forward in medical science.

Something to talk about

· How good are you at taking responsibility for the things you do?
· Is there something you need to own up to now?

Pray

Dear God, You know everything we've done before we tell anyone, please help us to have the courage to be honest about our actions. Amen.

Stand by me

Genesis 44:1–13 (but read the whole chapter if you can!)

'Joseph commanded the servant in charge of his house, "Fill the men's sacks with as much food as they can carry... Put my silver cup in the top of the youngest brother's sack, together with the money for his corn."... Early in the morning the brothers were sent on their way with their donkeys... Joseph said to the servant in charge of his house, "Hurry after those men. When you catch up to them, ask them, 'Why have you paid back evil for good? Why did you steal my master's silver cup?... You have committed a serious crime!'"

When the servant caught up with them, he repeated these words. They answered him, "... Sir, if any one of us is found to have it, he will be put to death, and the rest of us will become your slaves."

He said, "I agree; but only the one who has taken the cup will become my slave, and the rest of you can go free."... Joseph's servant searched carefully... and the cup was found in Benjamin's sack. The brothers tore their clothes in sorrow, loaded their donkeys, and returned to the city.'

Something to think about

Joseph has one last test for his brothers. They've come to see him with all kinds of gifts, but Joseph hides his special cup in Benjamin's bag and sends his servants after them to tell them they're thieves! Can you just imagine how sick they must have felt when they saw the cup in the sack?

Amazingly they all turn around with Benjamin and go back to the city. Years ago, they had turned their backs on Joseph as he had been taken in chains to Egypt. Not this time. This time they are standing with their brother, sticking by him to fight for him. What a transformation!

Bekah says...

When I was a teenager, I found my brother super annoying, but if I ever thought someone at school was being mean to him, I stood up for him. It turned out that even though he annoyed me, no one else was allowed to be unkind to him – because he was my brother and underneath it all, I loved him.

Something to talk about

· Has anyone ever stuck up for you?
· When have you stuck up for someone else?

Pray

Father God, thank You for always sticking by us. Please help us to be like You and stick by the people we love. Amen.

Sacrifice

Genesis 44:30–34

"'And now, sir," Judah continued, "if I go back to my father without the boy, as soon as he sees that the boy is not with me, he will die. His life is wrapped up with the life of the boy, and he is so old that the sorrow we would cause him would kill him. What is more, I pledged my life to my father for the boy. I told him that if I did not bring the boy back to him, I would bear the blame all my life. And now, sir, I will stay here as your slave in place of the boy; let him go back with his brothers. How can I go back to my father if the boy is not with me? I cannot bear to see this disaster come upon my father."'

Something to think about

Judah takes sticking up for his brother to a whole new level. He literally offers to step in and take his brother's place in prison. He really is taking responsibility for what happens. He doesn't want to see his brother go to prison, and he doesn't want to break his father's heart, so he is prepared to become a slave so that Benjamin can go home to his dad. That's pretty big love.

Did you know, Judah is the great, great, great (and a lot more 'great's) grandad of Jesus? You can see the family likeness. Jesus took our place on the cross so that one day we can go home to our heavenly Father.

Steve's amazing fact

During the Second World War, a German submarine fired a torpedo that struck an American troopship, the SS Dorchester. It was four chaplains who organised the soldiers in the panic. They handed out life jackets, but when they ran out, the chaplains gave theirs to other soldiers. The chaplains prayed with those unable to escape, and went down with the ship.

Something to talk about

• Has anyone ever stepped in to take your place to help you out of something?
• How did that make you feel?

Pray

Dear Jesus, it's just amazing that You took our place on the cross. We are so thankful for what You did for us, and what You still do for us. Amen.

God's plan

Genesis 45:1–5

'Joseph was no longer able to control his feelings in front of his servants, so he ordered them all to leave the room. No one else was with him when Joseph told his brothers who he was. He cried with such loud sobs that the Egyptians heard it, and the news was taken to the king's palace. Joseph said to his brothers, "I am Joseph. Is my father still alive?" But when his brothers heard this, they were so terrified that they could not answer. Then Joseph said to them, "Please come closer." They did, and he said, "I am your brother Joseph, whom you sold into Egypt. Now do not be upset or blame yourselves because you sold me here. It was really God who sent me ahead of you to save people's lives."'

Something to think about

Joseph can see that his brothers really have changed, and he gets pretty emotional as he tells them who he really is. Imagine how shocked they must have been! And imagine how scared they were, now they knew that this boy they had once treated so badly was now one of the most important men in the world.

But Joseph is incredibly kind and forgiving. Even now, after all this time and all that hurt, he can see that God has been at work in all their lives. And just like he has pointed the baker, the butler and even the king towards God, he tells his brothers that actually although they'd sold him, it was all part of God's amazing plan to save not just his family in the famine, but a whole country.

Steve says...

It drives me mad being stuck in traffic. It wastes so much time and is so inconvenient. So I try to make the most of it, relax and enjoy the 'me-time' by listening to a podcast or radio show. I'm not always great at it, but realising there is nothing you can do can create a sense of enforced chillaxing. And actually, it's what I really need.

Something to talk about
· When did you last have a conversation that made you all emotional?
· How good are you at having difficult conversations?

Pray
Father God, sometimes we don't understand Your way of doing things, but we trust that You always work for our good. Help us to continue trusting You. Amen.

Reunited

Genesis 45:14–15, 25–28

'He threw his arms round his brother Benjamin and began to cry; Benjamin also cried as he hugged him. Then, still weeping, he embraced each of his brothers and kissed them. After that, his brothers began to talk with him.

They left Egypt and went back home to their father Jacob in Canaan. "Joseph is still alive!" they told him. "He is the ruler of all Egypt!" Jacob was stunned and could not believe them.

But when they told him all that Joseph had said to them, and when he saw the wagons which Joseph had sent to take him to Egypt, he recovered from the shock. "My son Joseph is still alive!" he said. "This is all I could ask for! I must go and see him before I die."'

Something to think about

What a moment! Jacob has been left at home while his sons all go to Egypt, and he was scared they were never coming back. He was scared he and the rest of the household would starve, but now he has the best news ever.

Despite everything that has happened, all the hurt they have done to each other, the lies, the plotting and the pain, this family is reunited in love. There is one big, messy, teary hug. It's a beautiful thing, and it was only possible because every member of this family had been prepared to change, grow up, say sorry and forgive.

Steve's amazing fact

Canadian brothers Tommy Larkin and Stephen Goosney were put up for adoption when they were very young. They were taken in by separate families and grew up a few hundred miles apart. When they were 29 and 30, they tried looking for each other and realised something shocking: they now lived across the street from each other! They'd lived opposite each other and neither had known.

Something to talk about

· Is there someone you haven't spoken to for a while?
· What would need to happen for you to reunite?

Pray

Dear God, You are the God who loves to bring people together. Help us to always be ready to reunite with people. Amen.

Something for the weekend

Think about some family friends you haven't seen for a long time – you might not have fallen out them, just lost touch. Could you use this weekend to make some plans to spend time with them?

Baptised

Matthew 3:13–15

'At that time Jesus arrived from Galilee and came to John at the Jordan to be baptized by him. But John tried to make him change his mind. "I ought to be baptized by you," John said, "and yet you have come to me!"

But Jesus answered him, "Let it be so for now. For in this way we shall do all that God requires." So John agreed.'

Something to think about

We've jumped forward a long time in history now, from Joseph right up to the time that Jesus came to earth. We're picking up Jesus' story just as He's beginning to do the work that God sent Him to do. Up until now, Jesus was just living with His family, learning to be a carpenter like His earthly dad (a different Joseph!), and seeming to be very ordinary to most people as far as we know. But all that is about to change.

He starts by being baptised by His cousin John. Baptism was about being cleaned with water as a symbol that you wanted to make yourself clean enough for God. So John is confused when Jesus, the Son of God, wants to be baptised. He knows who Jesus is, and he knows Jesus is already good enough for God – surely He doesn't need to be baptised? But for Jesus, it's about showing that He's about to be good enough for everyone to know God.

Steve says...

People still get baptised today, not because it actually makes you clean or good enough for God, but to show all that God has done for you. It's a picture of God making you clean by giving you Jesus' goodness, and a way of showing that when you choose to follow Him you get a new life.

Something to talk about

· Have you been baptised or seen someone else get baptised?

· In what other ways can you also show you've started a new life with Jesus?

Pray

Dear Jesus, thank You that You came to be a human being just like us to give us new life. Please show us how You want us to live. Amen.

Loved

Matthew 3:16–17

'As soon as Jesus was baptized, he came up out of the water. Then heaven was opened to him, and he saw the Spirit of God coming down like a dove and alighting on him. Then a voice said from heaven, "This is my own dear Son, with whom I am pleased."'

Something to think about

This is a brilliant part of the story. Jesus is about to start on an exciting adventure, travelling around the country, telling people about God, healing people, feeding people and changing lives. It's going to be tough; there are people who aren't going to like what He does, who try to stop Him, who try to make out He's a fake, but here at the start of all that, something amazing happens. Jesus' Dad, God, sends His Holy Spirit to be with Jesus, and God tells Jesus and the world, 'This is my Son, I'm so pleased with Him.'

Knowing this, Jesus will have the strength to do anything that comes His way – because He knows who He is. He knows He is God's Son, and He knows God is pleased with Him and loves Him even before He's got to work!

Bekah says...

It really helps to remember that we belong to God as well, and to know how He feels about us. We can do that by spending time with Him, reading His Word and praying to Him. The more we know about what He thinks of us, the easier it is to face the hard times in our lives.

Steve's amazing fact

In 2017, one of the most searched for Bible verses was Jeremiah 29:11, "'For I know the plans I have for you,' declares the LORD, "plans to prosper you and not to harm you, plans to give you hope and a future'" (NIV). That must help a lot of people remember how God feels about them.

Something to talk about

· What do you think God says about you?
· How can you remember this when times are hard?

Pray

Dear God, thank You for choosing to love us like You love Jesus. When things are hard, help us to know we can do anything with Your Holy Spirit in us. Amen.

A hard place

Matthew 4:1–3

'Then the Spirit led Jesus into the desert to be tempted by the devil. After spending forty days and nights without food, Jesus was hungry. Then the devil came to him and said, "If you are God's Son, order these stones to turn into bread."'

Something to think about

It was a good job God had reminded Jesus who He was and sent Him His Holy Spirit – because the next thing that happens is that the Holy Spirit take Jesus into the desert to spend time praying and getting ready for what is happening next. Jesus is in a wild and lonely place with nothing to eat, and then the devil comes to make life even more difficult.

Cartoons make the devil look like a red character with pointy horns and a tail, but the truth is that one of the few things we know about him is that he is a liar – and he likes to convince us that he's just a cartoon character, harmless and not real at all. But this is a serious moment in Jesus' life and if the devil can persuade Him to do something wrong, it will wreck God's rescue plan for the world. Heaven must have been watching with bated breath to see what Jesus would do.

Bekah says...

There are some moments in our lives that could change everything, but we don't always see them as big or important. The decisions we make can shape our future, and it's important that we think about who we are listening to and being influenced by – God, or His enemy the devil.

Steve's amazing fact

If you read through the entire Bible, you'll see the number 40 crop up a lot. It appears so often that some people think it's particularly used to talk about times of difficulty or trouble.

Something to talk about

· When have you had to make a big decision that could change everything?
· What did you decide on and how did you do this?

Pray

Dear Father God, help us to hear Your voice louder than any other. Please show us how to stick to Your plan for our lives. Amen.

Hungry

Matthew 4:2–4

'After spending forty days and nights without food, Jesus was hungry. Then the Devil came to him and said, "If you are God's Son, order these stones to turn into bread."

But Jesus answered, "The scripture says, 'Human beings cannot live on bread alone, but need every word that God speaks.'"'

Something to think about

Forty days and nights without food – you would be seriously hungry after that! Jesus must have been too. Even though He was God, He was also a human. And as a human, He would have been very hungry. So when the devil comes along and suggests He turns a stone into some bread to eat, it would have been very tempting.

The truth is, making some bread isn't a bad thing to do – Jesus needed to eat. *But,* Jesus knows that God has always promised to provide for His people, and He needs to trust His Father to give Him what he needs and not try to magic it up on the devil's command. So He replies using a Bible verse to show the devil that He knows what He really needs is His Father.

Steve says...

There are often things we really need, but we need to get them the right way, not the wrong way. You might need to get your homework done, but not by copying someone else. We all need food, but not by taking a biscuit without asking. We need friends, but not by taking someone else's friend and leaving them out.

Bekah says...

Jesus must have been very hungry, and it's amazing that His attitude wasn't changed by it. Lots of people can get hangry - angry when they're hungry. I wonder if any of you suffer from hangriness?

Steve's amazing fact

Did you know that there have been some cases where people have survived for three days without water, and longer without food? No one is ever sure how long a person could survive – it's not the kind of experiment people volunteer for!

Something to talk about

· Have you ever gone the wrong way about getting something you needed?
· What would have been a better way?

Pray

Dear Lord Jesus, we're sorry for the times we have got things the wrong way and hurt people or disobeyed You. Please help us to trust You to provide what we need. Amen.

Prove it

Matthew 4:5–7

'Then the Devil took Jesus to Jerusalem, the Holy City, set him on the highest point of the Temple, and said to him, "If you are God's Son, throw yourself down, for the scripture says:
  'God will give orders to his angels about you;
  they will hold you up with their hands,
  so that not even your feet will be hurt on the stones.'"
Jesus answered, "But the scripture also says, 'Do not put the Lord your God to the test.'"'

Something to think about

This doesn't sound very tempting at all – the thought of jumping off a tall building is not very appealing! But that isn't the point of what the devil is trying to do here. He's questioning whether Jesus is who He says He is. It's like he wants Jesus to say 'God, if You meant what You said at my baptism, then prove it by sending Your angels to catch me.' But instead, Jesus answers with a Bible verse again, reminding the devil that you should never test God.

Sometimes we can try to test God in similar ways, not by jumping off skyscrapers, but by telling Him we'll believe in Him if does a big miracle, that we'll love Him is He gets us a new job, or we'll believe He's good if He heals someone we love. We often don't even realise we do it, but we make our love for God dependent on Him doing something we want.

Bekah says...

Jesus already knew that God loved Him and was pleased with Him, and that was enough. We need to be the same. Jesus died for us, and God tells us in the Bible that He loves us. Let's remember this when we're tempted to give God a demand in order to prove Himself.

Steve's amazing fact

The Kingdom Tower in Jeddah, Saudi Arabia is set to open in 2020. When it does, it will be the world's tallest skyscraper at a whopping 1,000 meters in height. The cost of the building's construction is estimated at $1.4 billion.

Something to talk about

· Have you ever wanted God to prove Himself to you?
· What helps you to know God is good even when times are hard?

Pray

Father God, thank You for loving us. Jesus, thank You for dying for us. Holy Spirit, help us to remember that we are loved and rescued, and to know that is enough. Amen.

Short cuts

Matthew 4:8–11

'Then the Devil took Jesus to a very high mountain and showed him all the kingdoms of the world in all their greatness. "All this I will give you," the Devil said, "if you kneel down and worship me."

Then Jesus answered, "Go away, Satan! The scripture says, 'Worship the Lord your God and serve only him!'"

Then the Devil left Jesus; and angels came and helped him.'

Something to think about

Wow, this is a pretty serious moment in history. Jesus had come to save the world, but to do that He was going to have to let people make up stories about Him, arrest Him and beat Him, and nail Him to a cross. Jesus is God, so He knew what was going to happen. But He was human too, so He would have been afraid of it happening.

The devil is trying to give Him a short cut. He's pretending that he can give Jesus the world if Jesus worships him. It might have seemed a much easier way to Jesus, but He knew it was wrong. He knew you should only worship God. Jesus was well aware that the devil couldn't really give Him the world but was just trying to make Jesus do something wrong, so He sends the devil away.

Bekah says...

Sometimes we can be tempted to worship or give all our time and energy to something other than God. Putting our focus on getting good grades or lots of money or even on our friends seems like an easier way to make ourselves happy. But truthfully, only God can give us true joy and peace, and we need to send the devil away when he tells us otherwise.

Something to talk about

· What things do you give lots of time and energy to?
· How much time and energy do you think you give to God?

Pray

Dear Father God, You are all we need, and we want to worship only You. Help us to see where we give too much time to other things and to focus on You instead. Amen.

Something for the weekend

Jesus replied to every temptation with a verse from the Bible – God's Word. Knowing your Bible is the easiest way to know God and remember who you are. So, why not write out some great Bible verses to put around your home to help you all stay true to God?

Humble happiness

Matthew 5:3–5

'Happy are those who know they are spiritually poor;
the Kingdom of heaven belongs to them!
Happy are those who mourn;
God will comfort them!
Happy are those who are humble;
they will receive what God has promised!'

Something to think about

After Jesus sends the devil away, He really starts to get going with the work He has to do. He travels the country doing amazing miracles and lots of people start to follow Him. Then He heads up a hill and begins to talk, but what He says seems surprising. Happy are those who are poor, sad and humble? It seems all upside down.

The thing is, Jesus knows that God's way is different to what the world says. He says, unless you are spiritually poor and humble enough to know that you need God, you won't be part of God's kingdom. When you think about it, it makes sense. If you think you're good enough by yourself, you won't let God in. If you do realise you're a bit broken and make mistakes, then you're going to want to ask God to help, and then you get to be part of His kingdom, which is great!

Bekah says...

I'm someone who loves to think I can fix everything and do anything. That sometimes means I forget to ask God to help me, or I avoid situations I think I can't handle. But when I stop and remember that I need God, it's so much better. I don't have to worry so much and I get to go on exciting new adventures with Him.

Steve's amazing fact

Nowadays, when people want help they often go to Google first! Some of the most asked questions in 2018 were: 'How do you...' 'do the floss dance?', 'bleed a radiator?', 'watch the Champions League?', 'delete Facebook?', 'put lights on a Christmas tree?', and 'solve a Rubik's cube?' I'm going to be honest – I googled that last one and it took me a long time to get it right even then.

Something to talk about

· When have you really known you needed God?
· How did He help you?

Pray

Father God, thank You for always being there. Please help us to remember we need You and not try to do everything on our own. Amen.

Good happiness

Matthew 5:6–9

'Happy are those whose greatest desire is to do what God requires;
God will satisfy them fully!
Happy are those who are merciful to others;
God will be merciful to them!
Happy are the pure in heart;
they will see God!
Happy are those who work for peace;
God will call them his children!'

Something to think about

Jesus keeps telling the people around Him what will bring them happiness, and it makes sense. People who want to do what God wants will get what they want – God doesn't say no to people who are trying to do His work on earth. Jesus says that His Father will show them mercy, which means showing kindness even when people don't deserve it and forgiving people who hurt you. Jesus promises that if you are kind and forgive, God will be kind and forgive you, and if you keep your heart pure, then you will see God one day!

Best of all – God loves peacekeepers. One of the names

for Jesus was 'Prince of Peace' (Isa. 9:6). Peacekeeping isn't for wimps. It's not about just keeping your head down; it takes guts and wisdom to be a peacekeeper. It might mean standing up for people who are being bullied, taking time to help friends or family work their problems out, or doing something you would rather not do. And it might mean biting your tongue and not getting into arguments; instead finding ways to understand what someone else is thinking.

Bekah says...

My younger brother and sister always used to fight in the car, so I always had to sit in the middle of the back seat so they couldn't hit each other. I didn't like being their peacekeeper!

Steve's amazing fact

The first United Nations (UN) peacekeeping mission took place in 1948. UN Peacekeeping troops are often called the 'blue helmets' because of their uniform, and they do a very important job in preventing many conflicts turning into full-scale wars by helping opposing parties to reach peaceful solutions through discussions and negotiation.

Something to talk about

· Who is the best peacekeeper in your family?
· What makes them so good? How can you help them out?

Pray

Dear God, we love that You are a God of peace. In a world that fights and argues so much, help us to bring peace to the people around us. Amen.

Stand-out happiness

Matthew 5:10–12

'Happy are those who are persecuted because they do what God requires;

the Kingdom of heaven belongs to them!

Happy are you when people insult you and persecute you and tell all kinds of evil lies against you because you are my followers. Be happy and glad, for a great reward is kept for you in heaven. This is how the prophets who lived before you were persecuted.'

Something to think about

Now this is a funny one. Happy are the *persecuted*. Do you know what persecuted means? It basically means bullied. How can that make you happy? Well, it's important to read the whole sentence – happy are people who are persecuted because they follow Jesus. That's slightly different. Jesus doesn't mean that the bullying will make you happy – that would just be weird, but if it's because you're following Jesus, it means you're standing out as someone special.

Jesus never promised that following Him would be easy. In fact He goes on to say some people will hate you. It's a bit like marmite – some people love it, some people hate it. Some people love Jesus, others hate Him and anyone who follows Him. But if you're following Him in a way that people notice, then that's good. It means you're doing well.

Bekah says...

In some countries, it's downright dangerous to be a follower of Jesus, but people choose to follow Him anyway because they know that being friends with Jesus is worth the risk of going to prison or even losing their lives.

Steve's amazing fact

Brother Andrew hadn't even completed high school, but God used him to do things that looked impossible. He smuggled Bibles into countries where it was dangerous to be a Christian. He could have found himself in a lot of trouble if he'd been caught, but God miraculously helped him to deliver Bibles across borders and past guards.

Something to talk about

· Have you ever been insulted or teased for following Jesus?
· What helps you be strong?

Pray

Dear Father God, we want to follow You, even if people don't always like it. Please help us to be courageous. Amen.

Sort it out!

Matthew 5:23–24

'So if you are about to offer your gift to God at the altar and there you remember that your brother has something against you, leave your gift there in front of the altar, go at once and make peace with your brother, and then come back and offer your gift to God.'

Something to think about

This talk of Jesus' is just full of good advice – He's talking to people who were Jewish, and were giving offerings to God in the synagogue to make themselves right with Him. Jesus is basically saying that before you go and fix things with God, go and fix things with anyone you have upset.

We can't be totally right with God if we're holding onto grudges, or if we haven't sorted out problems we've created by being unkind or rude. It's good to sort out problems quickly; not to let them grow and get worse.

Bekah says...

My Granny used to say we should keep a 'short account', which was basically the same thing. If she thought she'd upset someone, she'd check in and try to fix it, and she expected us to do the same! The other thing she taught me was to not go to bed angry with someone, but to sort out any arguments before I went to sleep so I could start the next day fresh and new. Pretty good advice.

Steve's amazing fact

After years of prejudice and persecution in South Africa, the Truth and Reconciliation Commission was set up in 1996 to help people face those who had mistreated them. Many, many people had a chance to build peace and forgiveness.

Something to talk about

· Do you tend to hold a grudge?
· Is there someone you need to sort things out with now?

Pray

Dear Lord Jesus, thank You for all Your great advice. Please help us to be good at saying sorry and fixing problems we have with others. Amen.

The extra mile

Matthew 5:39–42

'But now I tell you: do not take revenge on someone who wrongs you. If anyone slaps you on the right cheek, let him slap your left cheek too. And if someone takes you to court to sue you for your shirt, let him have your coat as well. And if one of the occupation troops forces you to carry his pack one kilometre, carry it two kilometres. When someone asks you for something, give it to him; when someone wants to borrow something, lend it to him.'

Something to think about

This is some great but difficult advice for peacekeeping. Jesus says don't take revenge – that's hard. When someone hurts us or cheats us, it's natural to want to hurt them back to even things up a bit. But Jesus says don't. It's not as straightforward as just letting people hurt you though – it's about quietly standing up to people without resorting to doing something wrong.

We can change the world if, when we come across evil, we respond with love. If everyone just keeps taking revenge, the world becomes a darker place with more and more nastiness all around. Responding with hate is normal, so when we respond with love, we'll stand out as carriers of God's love and light.

Bekah says...

I find this really hard. Growing up I loved to win an argument or prove someone wrong, or even get my own back. But as I've learned to follow Jesus, I've realised that love wins. When you just keep loving people, even when they're unkind, even when they're mean, even when they're trying to make you angry, they eventually are won over.

Steve says...

Mahatma Gandhi, a famous Indian lawyer, activist and writer once said, 'An eye for an eye only ends up making the whole world blind.' He's right. Just think about the repercussions of getting revenge - you might end up in trouble with a teacher or someone you work with, and where does revenge stop? It's much better to focus on the good things in your life and look at how you can move forward.

Something to talk about

· Have you ever got revenge on someone?
· When have you responded with love instead of hate?

Pray

Father God, thank You that You don't take revenge, that You love us even when we do things to hurt You. Help us to be more like You. Amen.

Love your enemies

Matthew 5:43–47

'You have heard that it was said, "Love your friends, hate your enemies." But now I tell you: love your enemies and pray for those who persecute you, so that you may become the children of your Father in heaven. For he makes his sun to shine on bad and good people alike, and gives rain to those who do good and to those who do evil. Why should God reward you if you love only the people who love you? Even the tax collectors do that! And if you speak only to your friends, have you done anything out of the ordinary?'

Something to think about

Jesus is taking His message one step further. This isn't just about not hurting your brother or sister if they hurt you. This is about loving your enemies. Your *enemies*. You might not even have enemies, but this is about the people you think deserve to be hated because of what they've done. People who have done really bad things.

It doesn't mean you have to become their best friend, or spend all your time with them. And it doesn't mean they're allowed to do wrong. But it does mean you let go of your hatred and pray for them instead. It means you don't gossip about them, or secretly hope they get their comeuppance. It's hard, but it's how Jesus treats us.

Bekah says...

I haven't really got any enemies but there have been some people in my life who have been very unkind to me. I've had bosses who were really difficult to work for and one of the things I've discovered is this: when you start to pray for these people in the way Jesus would, it changes how you feel about them. It helps you to love them like Jesus does.

Something to talk about

· Is there anyone you would consider to be an enemy?
· How can you pray for them today?

Pray

Dear Father God, You loved us even when we were Your enemies and didn't love You back. Please help us to love like You do. Amen.

Something for the weekend

Loving your enemies takes practice – why not look for some stories in the news, work out who the 'enemy' is in the story and then pray for them. Ask yourself: how would Jesus pray for them? Then do that.

Introductions

Galatians 1:1–3

'From Paul, whose call to be an apostle did not come from human beings or by human means, but from Jesus Christ and God the Father, who raised him from death. All the brothers and sisters who are here join me in sending greetings to the churches of Galatia:

May God our Father and the Lord Jesus Christ give you grace and peace.'

Something to think about

We've jumped forward a few more years to just after Jesus has died and risen again. Paul is an amazing follower of Jesus who has travelled all around the Mediterranean telling people about Jesus and starting new churches. This is a letter from him to a church in Galatia, a city in what we call Turkey.

Paul had started out trying to kill Christians. But then, he met Jesus on a road to Damascus, and that changed everything (Acts 9). He starts his letter by reminding the Galatians that he has this amazing job, travelling the world and talking about Jesus, because God asked him to. Not because he's anything special – it wasn't even his idea. Paul doesn't want anyone but God to get the praise for what he's doing. Pretty humble stuff.

Bekah says...

What do you want to do when you grow up? What do you think God has in store for you? Jeremiah 29:11 tells us that God has plans to give us hope and a future. The more we spend time with God and get to know Him, the more we'll get to learn what His brilliant plan is for our life – just like Paul.

Steve says...

When I was little I dreamt of becoming a farmer, before I changed my mind and decided on becoming a vet, then an astronaut, before settling on becoming a magician – which is what I am now. It just goes to show that dreams can come true with some determination, dedication and discipline.

Something to talk about

· Grown-ups – what did you want to be when you grew up? Has that changed?
· Children – what do you want to be when you grow up?

Pray

Father God, thank You for not just knowing us, but for having plans for our futures. Help us to listen to You so we can follow You closely. Amen.

Simple

Galatians 1:4–6

'In order to set us free from this present evil age, Christ gave himself for our sins, in obedience to the will of our God and Father. To God be the glory forever and ever! Amen.

I am surprised at you! In no time at all you are deserting the one who called you by the grace of Christ, and are accepting another gospel.'

Something to think about

There's a reason for Paul's letter – he's heard some news that's worrying him. He's heard that the Christians in this church have got confused about the amazing news that Jesus came and died to save them. Some other people have come along and told them some different things that make life much more complicated and difficult.

The truth is that following Jesus, becoming a Christian, is really simple. It just means believing that God loves you and created you, that He sent His Son Jesus to live on earth to rescue us. It just means understanding that the wrong things we do separate us from God, but that Jesus chose to die in our place so that we can be forgiven and be friends with God. All it takes is choosing to follow Jesus and saying sorry for doing things wrong. Simple.

Bekah says...

I became a Christian when I was a little girl. I was just four years old, and there was a lot I didn't understand about God, but I did know I wanted to be Jesus' friend - and that meant saying sorry for what I'd done wrong, and getting to know Him better by reading my Bible and praying.

Steve says...

My family weren't Christians so I didn't even hear much about knowing Jesus until I joined the Boys' Brigade (BB) when I was 12. At a BB Camp in Devon, I started to understand how He could be my very best friend, and I decided to follow Him from then onwards. It's one decision I have never regretted.

Something to talk about

· When did you become a Christian?
· Why did you choose to follow Jesus?

Pray

Dear God, thank You for doing all the hard work so that we can be friends with You. Please help us to follow You well all our lives. Amen.

Jobs for all

Galatians 2:6–9

'But those who seemed to be the leaders — I say this because it makes no difference to me what they were; God does not judge by outward appearances — those leaders, I say, made no new suggestions to me. On the contrary, they saw that God had given me the task of preaching the gospel to the Gentiles, just as he had given Peter the task of preaching the gospel to the Jews. For by God's power I was made an apostle to the Gentiles, just as Peter was made an apostle to the Jews. James, Peter, and John, who seemed to be the leaders, recognised that God had given me this special task; so they shook hands with Barnabas and me, as a sign that we were all partners. We agreed that Barnabas and I would work among the Gentiles and they among the Jews.'

Something to think about

When Paul was writing this letter, there were all sorts of people becoming Christians. Some of these had grown up in the Jewish faith (they were the Jews), and others had grown up in other religions (they were called the Gentiles).

Some of Paul's friends particularly liked telling the Jews about Jesus, but Paul loved talking to the Gentiles. Some people thought that made Paul's mates better than him – but Paul knew that was wrong. God wants us to talk to everyone, and He gives each of us different but equally important jobs to do – we're not all meant to do the same thing!

Bekah says...

Imagine if everyone had the same job! If everyone was a teacher, who would take care of you when you're sick or in trouble. Who would do the farming, or run the country, or build houses? It wouldn't work. It's easy to think some jobs are more important than others, but, really, we need everyone doing all kinds of things to make the world around us work.

Steve's amazing fact

Dwayne 'The Rock' Johnson is one of the highest paid actors in the world, and earned $124 million in 2018. It's no surprise that many people, young and old, dream about becoming actors!

Something to talk about

· What job would you hate to do?
· What jobs do people do that help you?

Pray

Father God, thank You for making us all different and for having a unique plan for each of us. Help us to value all the different jobs that people do. Amen.

Don't pretend

Galatians 2:11–14

'But when Peter came to Antioch, I opposed him in public, because he was clearly wrong. Before some men who had been sent by James arrived there, Peter had been eating with the Gentile brothers and sisters. But after these men arrived, he drew back and would not eat with the Gentiles, because he was afraid of those who were in favour of circumcising them. The other Jewish brothers and sisters also started acting like cowards along with Peter; and even Barnabas was swept along by their cowardly action. When I saw that they were not walking a straight path in line with the truth of the gospel, I said to Peter in front of them all, "You are a Jew, yet you have been living like a Gentile, not like a Jew. How, then, can you try to force Gentiles to live like Jews?"'

Something to think about

There's a load of confusing words here, but basically Peter was Paul's friend and another great follower of Jesus, and he'd been really happy talking to everyone from everywhere, until some other people came on the scene. Then he acted like he didn't even know his Gentile friends because he was so embarrassed to be with them!

God loves it when we act ourselves everywhere we go. He doesn't want us to feel like we have to pretend to be something we're not, and He certainly doesn't want us to ditch friends when someone better comes along.

Bekah says...

When I was a teenager, I sometimes found it hard to tell people at school that I went to church. I thought it was a bit embarrassing and I didn't want to tell them I followed Jesus. It turns out that when I did tell the truth, my friends just thought it was cool! I'd been worrying about nothing.

Steve's amazing fact

A teenager from China named Lui Shi Ching carried his friend, Lu Shao, to school every day for eight years. Lu Shao found it difficult to walk because of a congenital disorder, so his friend made the journey easier for him.

Something to talk about

· How easy do you find it talking to people about following Jesus?
· Is there someone you know you should tell about Jesus?

Pray

Dear Lord Jesus, You are an amazing friend to us – You never let us down. Help us to never let You down and to be truthful about our friendships with You. Amen.

Foolish

Galatians 3:1–3

'You foolish Galatians! Who put a spell on you? Before your very eyes you had a clear description of the death of Jesus Christ on the cross! Tell me this one thing: did you receive God's Spirit by doing what the Law requires or by hearing the gospel and believing it? How can you be so foolish! You began by God's Spirit; do you now want to finish by your own power?'

Something to think about

Paul is really quite frustrated with the Galatians. He's taught them of how the only thing that made it possible to be friends with Jesus was that He chose to die for us on the cross. But now they've listened to other people and made up a whole bunch of other things they should do to try to make themselves good enough for God. It's as though they think what Jesus did wasn't enough – that they have to do it themselves.

We live in a world where we often try to be 'enough'. We think we have to be good looking enough, clever enough, funny enough, thin enough, or good enough to have friends and be successful. And it's easy to think that God wants us to be good enough too.

Bekah says...

Social media can make life really tough. We might be always trying to get enough likes on our posts, or waiting to see if a picture gets enough comments on it for us to feel confident that people like us. It can be really exhausting. Thankfully, Jesus isn't like that. He just loves us – even when we're not funny, clever or good. That's quite a relief.

Steve's amazing fact

Did you know that in 2018 it was reported that there were 3.196 billion people using social media? That's up 13% from 2017. On average, every second, eleven new people started using social media, which is about one million people every day.

Something to talk about

· Do you ever feel like you need to meet certain requirements to be accepted somewhere?
· Why not take some time to tell each other what you love about each other, just as you are?

Pray

Father God, thank You so much for what You have done for us. Help us to know that is enough and to know that You love us just as we are. Amen.

Cursed?

Galatians 3:10–12

'Those who depend on obeying the Law live under a curse. For the scripture says, "Whoever does not always obey everything that is written in the book of the Law is under God's curse!" Now, it is clear that no one is put right with God by means of the Law, because the scripture says, "Only the person who is put right with God through faith shall live." But the Law has nothing to do with faith. Instead, as the scripture says, "Whoever does everything the Law requires will live."'

Something to think about

Hundreds of years before, God had given His people a whole load of laws to live by. They were good rules that helped people be kind, generous and even to rest, but Paul says that trying to keep all those laws is like living with a curse, which is pretty serious stuff!

What he means is that no human can keep all those laws and trying to do it is pretty stressful, especially if we think that's the only way to become good enough for God. When we really understand that Jesus already did all the hard work, we can relax. That doesn't mean we don't try to be kind and good, but we can know it doesn't all depend on us – it depends on Jesus.

Steve says...

When we look at the world around us, at school and at work, we can see how stressed people get trying to keep all the rules and trying to be successful, clever and cool. It's exhausting. How amazing it is that God has given us a way out through Jesus. How amazing it is that Jesus would love us so much that He died to make up for the things we do wrong.

Something to talk about

· Where or when do you feel pressured to be good enough?
· How does that make you feel?

Pray

Dear God, You are amazing for loving us so much. Thank You for taking away the need for us to try and do everything all by ourselves. Amen.

Something for the weekend

Take a few minutes to write down a list of things you don't have to worry about being good at to make God happy with you. Then, as a family, spend some time praying, thanking God for loving you all as you are.

Blessed

Galatians 3:13–14

'But by becoming a curse for us Christ has redeemed us from the curse that the Law brings; for the scripture says, "Anyone who is hanged on a tree is under God's curse." Christ did this in order that the blessing which God promised to Abraham might be given to the Gentiles by means of Christ Jesus, so that through faith we might receive the Spirit promised by God.'

Something to think about

There are some confusing words here again, but Paul is talking about that curse still, and he explains that Jesus took the curse away (the curse of trying to be good enough) when He died on the cross. Jesus took the 'punishment' people deserve for the things they have done wrong, and made them pure and blameless in the eyes of God. Paul explains that when that happened, we could all – absolutely everyone – have the blessing promised to Abraham all those years ago: knowing God and belonging to Him through Jesus. The promise that was given to Abraham, then Isaac, and then was stolen by Jacob, had now been fulfilled.

Bekah says...

It always blows me away when I think that perfect Jesus, who already had an amazing relationship with His Father God, should choose to take my curse and allow people to nail Him to a cross and kill Him. He didn't have to do that, no one made Him, but He chose to do it because He loves me, and you, so much.

Steve says...

Easter marks the death and resurrection of Jesus and is the most important of all the Christian festivals. This one weekend represents what was both brutally sad and totally incredible. Jesus was crucified, which meant He was nailed to a wooden cross and left to die, but then He rose again just three days later! The cross is a very important Christian symbol as it reminds us of what Jesus did for us by giving up His own life in order to save all those who follow and believe in Him.

Something to talk about

- What's the most amazing thing someone has done for you?
- How did that make you feel?

Pray

Father God, it's amazing that thousands of years after Abraham, Jesus fulfilled the promise, and that thousands of years later, people are still turning to Jesus. Thank You for all You have done for us. Amen.

Free to love

Galatians 5:13–15

'As for you, my brothers and sisters, you were called to be free. But do not let this freedom become an excuse for letting your physical desires control you. Instead, let love make you serve one another. For the whole Law is summed up in one commandment: "Love your neighbour as you love yourself." But if you act like wild animals, hurting and harming each other, then watch out, or you will completely destroy one another.'

Something to think about

It's true that we can't make ourselves good enough for God, and it's true that Jesus has done all the hard work for us on the cross and that makes us free to live amazing lives. But, as Paul reminds his friends, that doesn't mean we should start doing whatever we want. The laws God gave His people were His way of showing them how to live the best lives they could.

There were hundreds of laws, but Paul sums them up the same way Jesus did – love your neighbour the way you love yourself. That's a great tool to help you make decisions. You can ask: would I want someone to say this to me? Would I want them to do this to me? If the answer's yes, then it's probably OK to do. But if the answer's no, think again! God loves us and He wants us to love each other.

Steve says...

Loving each other is so much more than a fuzzy feeling – real love is in the things we do. My nephew knew this when he was very little. He saw me eating some chocolate and instead of asking for some he said, 'Shall we be friends?' It made me smile, and it's become our family's jokey way to ask for something, but it's great he knew that real friends share.

Steve's amazing fact

Married couples usually wear rings, but did you know why they're worn on the fourth finger of the left hand? It's because the ancient Greeks reckoned that this finger contained the 'vena amoris', the 'vein of love', running straight to the heart.

Something to talk about

· What would you love someone to do for you right now?
· How could you show that same love to someone?

Pray

Dear God, thank You for setting us free. You are so amazing. Please help us to use our freedom to do good things and to love people. Amen.

Good fruit

Galatians 5:22–26

'But the Spirit produces love, joy, peace, patience, kindness, goodness, faithfulness, humility, and self-control. There is no law against such things as these. And those who belong to Christ Jesus have put to death their human nature with all its passions and desires. The Spirit has given us life; he must also control our lives. We must not be proud or irritate one another or be jealous of one another.'

Something to think about

Jesus promised that if we choose to follow Him, He will send His Spirit to be with us, guide us and help us become more like Him. Following Jesus means letting His Spirit control our lives, and when that happens, we start behaving a certain way – and acting a lot like Him.

Paul gives us a list of what the Holy Spirit grows in us – some people call them the fruits of the Spirit. These are great character traits like love, joy, peace, patience and kindness. Wouldn't you love to be around people who are full of these things? And there's more: goodness is an obvious one, faithfulness means you stick by people, humility means you don't show off, and self-control means you think before you act and so stop yourself doing things you shouldn't. It's not just great to be around people like this, it's great to *be* like this.

Bekah says...

Growing up, I wanted to be great at singing and brilliant at speaking languages. But actually, as I've got older I have come to realise that the most important things in life aren't the skills I have; it's these fruits of the Spirit. I'd much rather spend time growing my kindness than my French skills, and it's much more useful.

Steve's amazing fact

In Southeast Asia, there is a plant called the durian, which has been called King of Fruits. But people either love it or hate it. There are those who think the custard-like pulp of the fruit is delicious, but then there are those who find its smell absolutely revolting.

Something to talk about

· Which of the fruits of the Spirit can you see in each other?
· Which ones would you like to grow a bit more?

Pray

Dear Holy Spirit, thank You for living in us. We want to let You grow these amazing fruits in our lives, so that we can be more like Jesus. Amen.

Help each other

Galatians 6:1–2

'My friends, if someone is caught in any kind of wrongdoing, those of you who are spiritual should set him right; but you must do it in a gentle way. And keep an eye on yourselves, so that you will not be tempted, too. Help to carry one another's burdens, and in this way you will obey the law of Christ.'

Something to think about

Now this is tricky. Paul is a long way from his friends, and he is trying to help them grow and be the best they can be – but this bit of advice needs handling carefully. He's reminding his friends in Galatia to help each other be good and to become more like Jesus, and he's suggesting that they tell each other when they see each other do something wrong – but they need to do this *gently*.

It's very easy to criticise each other and point out each other's mistakes, but that's not what Paul is talking about. He's talking about having a gentle conversation with the aim of trying to help someone be better, not just making them feel worse. Paul also says to watch out for what you're doing, too.

Bekah says...

When I was a teacher, some children loved to point out everything that their friends did wrong: 'Miss, Susi's using the wrong pencil,' 'Miss, Tom hasn't underlined the title,' or 'Miss, Hannah's picking her nose!' Gross! I really didn't want to know, and they really weren't trying to be helpful; they were just trying to get people in trouble.

Steve says...

A few years ago I climbed Mount Kilimanjaro, the highest mountain in Africa. At 5,895 metres high, there's even snow at the top. It was quite an experience, but one I'd never have achieved without the help of the guides and porters. There were actually two or three porters per hiker, and two guides for every four hikers. This and the amazing support equipment kept us safe on the mountain.

Something to talk about

· Is there something that you think you need to stop doing?
· How can your family help you?

Pray

Dear Lord Jesus, thank You for wanting us to be the best we can be. Please help us to be good at listening to others and helping them. Amen.

Be honest

Galatians 6:3–5

'You should each judge your own conduct. If it is good, then you can be proud of what you yourself have done, without having to compare it with what someone else has done. For we each have our own load to carry.'

Something to think about

It's very easy to go through life thinking we're perfect, but Paul says, think again. Think again and be really honest with yourself. Are there some parts of your life that aren't perfect? Perhaps you're not very patient with your brother or sister. Maybe you hide when someone wants you to help with the washing up. Or is it that you get angry really easily?

It's not about always looking at our faults and feeling bad though, and it's definitely not about comparing ourselves to other people and thinking we're not as good. It's OK to recognise where we're doing well – it's just about being honest. Honest about where we're getting it right, and honest about where we're not. And then asking God to work in us to get more right. He'll never say no to that!

Bekah says...

We have five girls and it's really easy for them to compare themselves to each other, but the truth is they're all so different. One is great at dancing, another at maths, another is a brilliant designer and cake maker, and another is brilliant with young children. We've taught them to focus on their own things and their own development. If they start trying to compare their weaknesses with their sisters' strengths, they get sad and it's totally unnecessary.

Steve's amazing fact

We all have strange talents, and I thought my memory was pretty amazing until I checked out the competition at the 2nd Asia Pacific Memory Championship in 2018. One of the kids' competitors, Tang Binjia, memorised a sequence of a deck of playing cards in just 16.434 seconds, breaking the children's world record.

Something to talk about

· What have you done that you're really proud of?
· What would you like to be better at?

Pray

Father God, thank You for making us unique. Please help us to remember that You don't want us to be like anyone else, just to be more like You. Amen.

Gardening

Galatians 6:7–10

'Do not deceive yourselves; no one makes a fool of God. People will reap exactly what they sow. If they sow in the field of their natural desires, from it they will gather the harvest of death; if they sow in the field of the Spirit, from the Spirit they will gather the harvest of eternal life. So let us not become tired of doing good; for if we do not give up, the time will come when we will reap the harvest. So then, as often as we have the chance, we should do good to everyone, and especially to those who belong to our family in the faith.'

Something to think about

Whether you love gardening or hate it, there's a basic rule: if you plant a pea, you grow a pea plant; if you plant a peanut, you grow a peanut plant; if you plant a sunflower seed, you grow a sunflower plant. You get the idea.

That's what Paul is talking about here. Except he's not really talking about plants, he's talking about our lives. He says if you spend time with God – praying, going to church, reading the Bible – you'll grow those fruits of the Spirit we talked about, and you'll be close to Him. If you spend your time doing whatever you want and hurting people, you'll grow in selfishness and hate and will get further away from God.

You harvest what you plant. You can't plant greed and grow kindness – it just doesn't work like that. So be careful what you plant.

Steve's amazing fact

Some seeds grow really quickly. A certain type of bamboo has been known to grow up to 91cm a day. And apparently, the slowest-growing tree in the world is a White Cedar in Canada. It has only grown 10cm in 55 years.

Something to talk about

· How important is spending time with God to you?

· How can you grow as a follower of Jesus?

Pray

Dear Father God, we want to grow beautiful things in our lives, and we know that all those things come from You. Help us to stay close to You. Amen.

Something for the weekend

Why not visit a garden centre or supermarket and buy a plant or some seeds to grow? As you take care of your plant over the coming months and years, you could think about how you can grow the fruits of the Spirit in your lives.

Bring your family together again!

Continue your daily, shared experience of the Bible with *All Together* and *Time Together*.

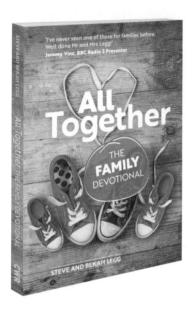
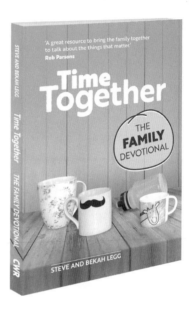

All Together

Discover more of the Bible together – from Creation, Moses, The Ten Commandments and Esther, to the birth, life and resurrection of Jesus.

ISBN: 978-1-78259-692-9

Time Together

Discover the stories of Noah, Abraham, Ruth, King David and others as well as a closer look at the Psalms, the Christmas story, and people in the Bible who encountered Jesus.

ISBN: 978-1-78259-798-8

For more information, current prices and to order visit **cwr.org.uk/shop** or call **01252 784700.**
Also available from Christian bookshops.

Bible reading notes designed especially
for each member of the family

With six different titles available as one-year subscriptions, you and everyone in your family can be inspired on their own faith journey every day of the year. Choose your way of engaging with the Bible:

- **Insightful and encouraging** Bible reading notes for men and women
- **Practical and relevant** daily guidance for teenagers
- **Fun and engaging** daily readings for children

| Every Day with Jesus | Inspiring Women Every Day | Life Every Day (Jeff Lucas) | Mettle 15–18s | YP's 11–14s | Topz 7–11s |

For more information, current prices and to order a one-year subscription, visit **cwr.org.uk/subscriptions** or call **01252 784700**.
Also available from Christian bookshops.

For young readers aged 3–6, the Pens series helps introduce Bible reading and prayer in a colourful and accessible way.
Visit our website for more information.